The Economics
of Foreign Aid
and Self-Sustaining
Development

Also of Interest

Energy in the Transition from Rural Subsistence, edited by Miguel S. Wionczek, Gerald Foley, and Ariane van Buren

Interdependence in a World of Unequals: African-Arab-OECD Cooperation for Development, edited by Dunstan Wai

Threat to Development: Pitfalls of the NIEO, William Loehr and John P. Powelson

The Economics of New Technology in Developing Countries, edited by Frances Stewart and Jeffrey James

Development Financing: A Framework for International Financial Cooperation, edited by Salah Al-Shaikhly

International Financial Cooperation: A Framework for Change, Frances Stewart, Arjun Sengupta, and Salah Al-Shaikhly

Finance and Development: The Role of International Commercial Banks in the Third World, Michael Da Costa

U.S. Foreign Aid: An Assessment of New and Traditional Development Strategies, Elliott R. Morss and Victoria A. Morss

The Challenge of Integrated Rural Development in India: A Policy and Management Perspective, Gerald E. Sussman

Managing Development in the Third World, Coralie Bryant and Louise G. White

From Dependency to Development: Strategies to Overcome Underdevelopment and Inequality, edited by Heraldo Muñoz

Appropriate Technology for Development: A Discussion and Case Histories, edited by Donald D. Evans and Laurie Nogg Adler

Dependency and Marxism: Toward a Resolution of the Debate, edited by Ronald H. Chilcote

Agroclimate Information for Development: Reviving the Green Revolution, edited by David F. Cusack

Technology Transfer and Development: India's Hindustan Machine Tools Company, R. C. Mascarenhas

*Available in hardcover and paperback.

Westview Special Studies in Social, Political, and Economic Development

The Economics of Foreign Aid and Self-Sustaining Development

Raymond F. Mikesell

in association with Robert A. Kilmarx and Arvin M. Kramish

The principal purpose of this book is to apply economic development theories and the findings of empirical studies to major issues of U.S. foreign aid policy. The authors address such questions as: 1) Is there a conflict between maximizing economic growth on the one hand and reducing absolute poverty or satisfying basic needs on the other? 2) What is the role of foreign aid in promoting growth at different stages in the development process, and how can aid be more effective in promoting self-sustained growth? 3) What should be the role of government in promoting development, and how do government policies inhibit the effectiveness of foreign aid? 4) How should the limited supplies of foreign aid be allocated among countries at different stages of development, among sectors within countries, and between private and public activities?

Drawing on a large number of empirical studies of individual countries, Dr. Mikesell and his associates conclude that government policies that provide incentives to the free market are the most closely associated with development success. This suggests that foreign aid programs should be designed to encourage indigenous private forces of economic progress rather than concentrate on financing government infrastructure projects.

Dr. Raymond F. Mikesell is W. E. Miner Professor of Economics at the University of Oregon. He has been a senior economist in the U.S. Department of the Treasury and was on the senior staff of the Council of Economic Advisors, Executive Office of the President. Robert A. Kilmarx is president of Management International Analysis Consultants and a former director of research at the Center for Strategic and International Studies, Georgetown University. Arvin M. Kramish is a private consultant in international trade investments and former deputy vice president of Overseas Private Investment Corporation.

The Economics
of Foreign Aid
and Self-Sustaining
Development

Raymond F. Mikesell
in association with Robert A. Kilmarx
and Arvin M. Kramish

Westview Press / Boulder, Colorado

Westview Special Studies in Social, Political, and Economic Development

Published in 1983 in the United States of America by
   Westview Press, Inc.
   5500 Central Avenue
   Boulder, Colorado 80301
   Frederick A. Praeger, President and Publisher

Library of Congress Catalog Card Number 82-51311
ISBN 0-86531-577-9

Composition for this book was provided by the author
Printed and bound in the United States of America

Contents

Preface

This study was prepared under a US Government contract for the Departments of State and Treasury and the Agency for International Development. The views and conclusions contained in this study should not be interpreted as representing the opinion or policy of the US Government. However, I benefitted greatly from meetings on successive drafts of this study with members of a monitoring committee consisting of representatives from the three sponsoring agencies. My associates in this project, Robert A. Kilmarx and Arvin M. Kramish, also attended these meetings and assisted me in taking account of the views expressed on major issues addressed at these meetings. They also assisted me in obtaining important documents from Washington-based development assistance agencies and in arranging interviews with representatives of these agencies. Finally, a substantial portion of the literature review on economic development was conducted by Michael Hutchison, a Ph.D. candidate in economics at the University of Oregon.

Raymond F. Mikesell

Introduction

The Work Statement accompanying the government contract under which this study was prepared called for a review and evaluation of the literature on economic development with special reference to the extent and conditions under which foreign aid can assist countries in achieving economic development on a self-sustaining basis without need for continuous concessionary aid flows. The Contractor was also requested to investigate the conditions under which foreign aid has contributed positively to achieving this goal. Finally, the Contractor was asked to address certain policy issues relating to development strategy and the role of foreign aid in the promotion of development strategy. The content and approach of this study, therefore, reflects our efforts to deal with the conceptual problems and policy issues outlined in the Work Statement and to bring to bear the available empirical evidence on certain of these issues.

Throughout the post-World War II period foreign aid by governments and by multilateral institutions financed by governments has been closely associated with the economics of development. Except for emergency assistance following disasters that have left people starving or homeless, foreign aid has had as its ultimate purpose the promotion of development rather than providing a temporary subsidy to consumption. Foreign aid policies have been strongly influenced by the thinking of development economists, and this thinking has changed over the decades since World War II as we have learned more about the development process. A review of the theoretical approaches to development by economists and of their analysis of the development process over the past quarter century provides background for evaluating the objectives and effectiveness of current foreign aid programs. In addition, some of the approaches and goals of development assistance cannot be fully appreciated without some knowledge of how they originated and the circumstances surrounding their emergence.

Chapter 1 provides a brief history of development theories and the rationale for aid, beginning with the earlier capital-oriented theories and ending with the emergence of the emphasis on outward-looking economic policies for the achievement of growth. Chapter 2 discusses the shift in the emphasis of some development economists and foreign aid practitioners from growth to the meeting of basic human needs. In these first two chapters we do not distinguish among the several types of development assistance other than to identify such assistance as originating from public donors, either bilateral or multilateral. In Chapter 3 we examine the forms and conditions of foreign assistance and define "concessionary aid" with which this study is primarily concerned. In Chapter 4 we seek to define more precisely the concept of self-sustaining growth, which is regarded by the Work Statement as the principal goal of concessionary aid. Chapter 5 outlines an approach to assessing the contribution of concessionary aid to economic growth, while Chapter 6 marshalls some of the empirical evidence on the effectiveness of different types of foreign aid programs on various economic sectors of developing countries. The final chapter presents certain conclusions with respect to the development process and the criteria for evaluating the effectiveness of foreign aid in promoting the indigenous economic forces for growth. The specific issues addressed reflect those set forth in the Work Statement for the preparation of this report.

1
Development Theory, Foreign Economic Assistance and Growth: A Brief History

THE BRETTON WOODS APPROACH TO DEVELOPMENT ASSISTANCE

Foreign aid for economic development is mainly a phenomenon of the post-World War II period. However, US governmental interest in economic assistance to developing countries goes back to the last century. The first International Conference of American States adopted a resolution on April 14, 1890 recommending the establishment of an International American Bank, and President Harrison recommended to Congress the incorporation of such a bank.[1] European colonial powers were, of course, concerned with assisting economic development in their dependent territories throughout the 19th and 20th Centuries, and much of their economic assistance to the new independent states formed after World II constituted a continuation of their development and other economic assistance during the colonial period.

According to its charter formulated at the Bretton Woods conference in 1944, the World Bank had the dual function of promoting the reconstruction of the war-torn countries, both developed and developing, and of promoting economic development in the less developed countries.[2] The concept of development assistance embodied in the Articles of Agreement for the World Bank was that of promoting the flow of private international capital in the form of both loans and direct investments to developing countries. Because of the political constraints on this flow, the Bank's operations were designed to supplement the normal flow of capital by making or participating in direct loans out of its paid-in capital or out of funds borrowed by the Bank, or by guaranteeing in whole or in part loans made by private investors. Originally it was expected that guaranteeing loans made by private investors would constitute a major activity of the Bank, but this approach was abandoned in favor of direct Bank lending. However, before making a loan the Bank must be "satisfied that

in the prevailing market conditions the borrower would
be unable otherwise to obtain the loan under conditions
which in the opinion of the Bank are reasonable for the
borrower."3

In the early days of its history the Bank's policy
was to make loans for specific projects in developing
countries that met the Bank's conditions for creditworthiness and for self-help measures that emphasized fiscal
and monetary responsibility. The World Bank got off
to a slow start in making loans to developing countries,
in large part because of its conservative policies. In
the first six fiscal years to June 30, 1952, the Bank
made development loans totalling only $885 million of
which $329 million went to Latin America, $129 million
to Asia and the Middle East, and $125 million went to
Africa; the remainder went to Europe and Australia.
The position of Eugene Black, President of the World
Bank from 1949 to 1962, was that the function of foreign
aid is to promote and marginally supplement the flow of
private loan and direct investment capital to the
developing countries and to assist these countries in
mobilizing their own resources for achieving their
development goals. The idea that a large annual flow
of public external financing was required for initiating
economic growth in the developing world was not accepted
by either the World Bank or the US Government during
the 1950s.

During the early post-World War II period US
bilateral assistance for development, as contrasted
with our substantial rehabilitation and reconstruction
aid to the developing countries of the Far East and
other areas, consisted mainly of Export-Import Bank
loans that served both to provide project assistance
and to promote US exports. US bilateral assistance for
development was gradually expanded under President Truman's Point IV program announced in 1949, but the
volume of assistance was small. The Point IV program
was based on a belief that technical assistance could
make a major impact on economic development abroad
without significant amounts of capital assistance. The
Point IV program included efforts to encourage private
foreign investment through a program of political risk
guarantees on US foreign investments and the negotiation
of investment treaties to improve the climate for foreign
investment. The program also involved an expansion of
loans for economic development by the Export-Import Bank.

THE DEMAND FOR LARGE AMOUNTS OF GLOBAL AID

The emergence of economic nationalism in Latin
America and in the developing countries that became
independent during the 1950s and 1960s was accompanied
by a growing demand for large amounts of foreign assist-

ance from industrialized countries for the promotion
of economic growth. Following political independence,
economic growth as measured by the percentage increase
in per capita national income became the primary political objective of the developing countries. These
countries rejected both the project-bankable loan approach of the World Bank and the technical assistance
and direct foreign investment approaches of the US
government in favor of large global aid programs to be
administered by the United Nations with few, if any,
strings attached. The UN Secretariat played an important role in articulating these demands, while much of
the economic and social rationale was supplied by
social scientists in the developed countries. In a
report by a group of experts to the Secretary General
of the UN issued in 1951, estimates were made of the
total capital required by all developing countries to
support an annual rate of growth in per capital national
incomes of 2 percent over the 1950-1960 period. Of
the total annual requirements of $19 billion, it was
estimated that $5 billion could be met by domestic
saving, leaving about $14 billion per year to be covered
by foreign capital.[4]

Since the latter amount was believed to be well in
excess of what could be attracted from private sources,
it was argued that much of this capital must come from
foreign governments and multinational agencies in the
form of grants and other concessional aid.[5]

The economic rationale or theoretical underpinnings
for the global external capital requirements put forth
in the early 1950s were rather crude, but a number of
capital-oriented development models were formulated by
economists during the 1950s and 1960s, which provided a
certain scientific respectability to the estimation of
these requirements for the developing world as a whole.
One of the important underpinnings for the external
capital requirements was supplied by Walter Rostow's hypothesis of the "take-off into self-sustaining growth."
Rostow's concept of the "take-off" caught the imagination
of the world's economists and became part of the standard
lexicon of foreign aid policy makers and development economists in the late 1950s and 1960s, but its popularity
subsided with a better understanding of the development
process in the 1970s.

Rostow's Concept of the Take-Off
Into Self-Sustaining Growth

Rostow's familiar historical stage development hypothesis envisaged the following stages: (1) the traditional society; (2) the long period during which economic
and social preconditions for growth are evolved; (3)
the relatively short period of the take-off into self-
sustaining growth; (4) the rapid rise to maturity;

and (5) the era of high mass consumption, or alterna-
tively, high social investment in military and space
machinery.[6] The key argument in Rostow's approach
is found in his concept of the take-off as a unique
stage in historical development which requires the
following three related conditions: (1) a rise in
productive investment, say, from 5 percent or less to
over 10 percent of national income; (2) the development
of one or more manufacturing sectors with a high rate
of growth; and (3) the existence or rapid emergence of a
political, social and institutional framework conducive
to the transmission of impulses to expansion throughout
the economy, including the capacity to mobilize capital
from domestic sources. This third condition is necessary
for the growth process to be self-enforcing, since unless
the income and savings from a leading sector are trans-
mitted to other sectors-particularly manufacturing, but
also to modernization of agriculture and other sectors
of the economy--there cannot be general and sustained
rises in productivity and output. Rostow proceeded to
identify the period of the take-off for a number of
countries such as Great Britain (1783-1802), the US
(1843-1860), Germany (18501873), and Japan (1878-1900).
These periods of takeoff have been almost universally
criticized by economic historians who found little or
no evidence for any of the unique periods described by
Rostow.[7]

Rostow suggested that domestic savings during the
take-off period could be supplemented by capital imports
so as to increase the level of investment required for
the increase in the growth rate. It was this aspect of
the take-off hypothesis that was seized upon by a number
of development economists to justify the provision of
large amounts of aid to initiate the take-off process
and assure the rapid achievement of self-sustaining
growth. Unfortunately, many development economists
seemed to have forgotten the preconditions for the take-
off originally specified by Rostow and sought to apply
the take-off hypothesis to a large number of developing
countries that were far from having attained these preconditions.

The Balanced Growth and
Big Push Hypotheses

The functions of foreign aid were broadened by some
development economists to include a hastening of the
preconditions for the achievement of sustained growth.
These preconditions were to be created by massive infusions of aid for infrastructure, without much attention
being paid to the social and institutional changes that
required centuries before the present developed countries reached Rostow's take-off stage. The case for
promoting development on all fronts emerged from the

"balanced growth theory" which suggested that if all sectors, including industry, agriculture, infrastructure and human skill development, could grow at relatively rapid rates at the same time, the conditions for the take-off could be achieved without the long historical period experienced by the older developed countries. This approach was formally developed as the theory of the "big push" by Paul Rosenstein-Rodan in a series of articles in the early 1960s.[8]

Critics of the balanced growth and "big push" doctrines (of whom Albert O. Hirschman is perhaps the best known) deny both the necessity of balanced growth as a condition for growth and its feasibility and realism as a theory of development.[9] Hirschman argued that growth proceeds by a process of induced investment in which one sector of the economy or industry moves ahead in response to certain inducements, and in turn induces investments in other sectors or industries. The concept of a "big push" involving a simultaneous investment in a large number of industries and overhead capital financed by a large influx of foreign aid was rejected as inconsistent with the development process. How do you suddenly transform an economy by means of massive and simultaneous investments on all fronts without providing the skills, managerial experience and ability, the changes in social structure and attitudes, and other concomitants of development?

Several economists objected that for many underdeveloped countries there were severe limits on how much external capital could be utilized productively, or "absorbed," as a consequence of low skill levels, lack of managerial talent, and poor governmental administrative facilities.[10] However, other economists were convinced that large infusions of external capital and technical assistance could achieve the preconditions for self-sustaining growth.

DEVELOPMENT OPTIMISM AND FOREIGN AID
MODELS OF THE 1960s

During the 1960s the approach of the World Bank and of the Eisenhower Administration to development assistance was abandoned in favor of a commitment on the part of the US and other developed countries to provide large amounts of concessionary aid directed to supporting comprehensive development plans. The new approach was accompanied by a high degree of optimism that most of the world's underdeveloped countries could be elevated to a condition of self-sustaining growth within a generation or so, and the UN and other international agencies disseminated estimates of global aid required to achieve growth targets in the developing world. This development optimism and dedication of the governments of developed countries to providing substantial amounts of development assistance found economic justification in capital-oriented growth models broadly accepted by most of the world's leading development economists.

In 1963 the UN Secretariat made a projection of the foreign exchange gap of developing countries that must be filled if these countries were to achieve a 5 percent growth in GDP for the period 1950-1960 based on import requirements to sustain the required level of invest-ment.[11] In the course of an address to the Development Assistance Committee (DAC) of the OECD in July 1965, the President of the World Bank, George D. Woods, suggested that "between now and 1970 the less developed countries might productively use an additional $3-$4 billion per year."

Since this was in addition to the approximately $10 billion in annual net flow of public and private finan-cial resources from DAC countries to developing coun-tries, the Bank's estimate of the amount of external capital which developing countries might "productively use" was on the order in magnitude of $13 to $14 billion per year.[12] The World Bank's estimate of additional aid requirements was not based on a growth model, but rather on a review of the public and private investment programs of the developing countries that met certain standards of technical and economic feasibility. By the mid-1960s there were a number of estimates of external capital re-requirements for the developing countries put forward by international agencies, all of which were in excess of current financial flows from private and public sources. The wide acceptance of global "gap" approaches to foreign aid requirements led to a recommendation by the DAC that each member devote 1 percent of its national income to development assistance (including net private flow).[13] This goal was in line with a resolution adopted by the United Nations Conference on Trade and Development (UNCTAD) in 1964. The 1 percent target was not based on any agreed estimate of "requirements" however deter-mined, but was simply a politically determined donors' goal which DAC has continued to exhort its members to achieve to the present time, but without much in the way of credible rationale.

President Kennedy set forth ambitious goals for the US for accelerating the growth of the developing countries and pledged the US government to a leading role in achieving self-sustaining growth in most of the developing world. But it was during the Johnson Administration that US bilateral aid (in real terms) for promoting economic growth in the LDCs reached a zenith.

The Chenery-Strout Two-Gap Model

US foreign assistance programs were heavily influenced by a foreign aid model formulated by Hollis B.
Chenery and Alan M. Strout, who held leading positions
on the policy staff of AID.[14] The Chenery-Strout two-
gap model combined three strains of thinking of economists for estimating foreign aid requirements. These
were (1) the skill limitation (essentially the capital
absorptive capacity approach); (2) the gap between
domestic investment required to achieve a given rate of
economic growth and domestic savings; and (3) the gap
between foreign exchange requirements to sustain the
required level of domestic investment and the country's
foreign exchange earnings. A country's progress toward
the goal of self-sustaining growth at given target
rates could be constrained during different periods or
phases (not necessarily in any particular order) by (a)
the skill limitation; (b) the savings limitation; or
(c) the foreign exchange limitation. It was argued
that foreign aid could play a role in relieving each of
these constraints and could promote the level of investment necessary to achieve eventual self-sustaining
growth. The operation of the model for any particular
country assumed the existence of a positive marginal
propensity to save which would eventually yield the
critical level of domestic savings to finance the
required investment, and a rate of growth of exports in
excess of the import growth rate, so that exports would
eventually rise sufficiently to overcome any foreign
exchange constraint. In addition, countries would need
to take appropriate measures with the help of foreign
technical and other assistance to remove the internal
obstacles to raising investment to the required level.
Although the Chenery-Strout model was capital oriented,
it fully recognized the need for governmental policies
that would promote productivity, savings, and the allocation of resources to productive investment. Where
the skill level was too low to permit a level of investment sufficient to achieve the target rate of growth,
foreign aid, including technical assistance, served to
increase the capacity of a country to employ capital
productively.

The Chenery-Strout model became exceedingly popular
and was broadly used as a basis for both the administration of foreign aid programs in individual countries
and the estimation of global aid requirements. In the
basic model, the capital-output ratio was fixed, although
the authors recognized that it would change over time
with increases in productivity. However, by making
capital the independent variable and output the dependent
variable in a Harrod-Domar type model, capital became
the primary engine of growth.[15] Thus, if the rate of
investment were 9 percent and the capital output-ratio

was 3, the rate of growth of output would be 3 percent per annum. If foreign capital supplemented domestic investment so that the investment ratio rose to 12 percent, the growth rate would increase by 1 percent to 4 percent.

The Chenery-Strout two-gap foreign aid model has been widely criticized on several grounds. One criticism has to do with the assumptions of the model regarding the relationship between output and international trade implied in the foreign exchange constraint and another relates to the dominant role given to capital inputs in the growth process. The possibility of an ex ante foreign exchange gap which is different from an ex ante savings investment gap rests on the assumption of relative inelasticity between imported and domestic inputs for production and the assumption that exports are not readily expandable. If imported and domestic inputs are relatively substitutable or if exports are responsive to price adjustments, there can be no difference in the ex ante gap except in the short run.[16] With regard to the dominant role given to capital inputs, statistical studies of actual growth based on other models, such as the Cobb-Douglass model, have not found support for attributing an increase in the growth rate almost entirely to an increase in capital inputs. This point will be illustrated later on.

CRITICISM OF CAPITAL-ORIENTED GROWTH MODELS

The Chenery-Strout foreign aid model has been widely criticized, mainly on the basis of its assumptions and the dominant role given to capital in the growth process. Statistical studies of actual growth based on other models, such as a Cobb-Douglass model, have rarely found support for attributing such a high proportion of the increase in the growth rate to the increase in capital inputs. This point will be illustrated later on.

Another criticism relates to the assumption of the model that capital inflow from concessionary or nonconcessionary sources necessarily constitutes a net addition to domestic capital investment. A net inflow of resources will not necessarily take the form of an equal amount of increase in domestic investment, no matter how carefully the foreign aid donor may seek to tie the resources he provides to particular investment projects or activities. Resources are fungible, and aid for a particular project may simply take the place of domestic capital that would otherwise have been used for that project, with the result that the aid simply increases domestic consumption or, perhaps, acquisition of military hardware. Finally, the savings function employed in the Chenery-Strout model, which is essentially the Keynesian savings hypothesis based on the existence of a marginal propensity to save that is higher than the average propensity to save, has been rejected by a number of economists in favor of other types of savings functions such as the Friedman permanent income hypothesis or the Modigliani life-cycle hypothesis. Also statistical studies do not bear out the assumption that the average savings rate increases with the growth in per capita income.[17]

The Savings Rate and Capital Imports

A number of economic treatises have not only attacked the basic assumptions of the capital-oriented foreign aid models, but have suggested that, in some countries at least, foreign aid might impair rather than promote long-term growth.[18] This aid pessimism is based in part on statistical findings that foreign aid for development does not simply add an equivalent amount to total investment, but is partly or even largely consumed (depending upon the data employed and the statistical methodology) and thereby reduces the savings rate.[19] One of the reasons given for a reduction in the savings rate is that foreign aid enables governments to shift some of their expenditures from investment projects financed by foreign aid to social programs, or to reduce taxes. Another argument is that to the extent that savings are a function of investment opportunities, as suggested by Houthakker,[20] and that some opportunities are preempted by foreign capital, capital flows will be offset in part by a decline in domestic savings. On the other hand it has been argued that some investment opportunities are created by foreign aid.

Even though some of the foreign aid resources are consumed (and it would be surprising if they did not add directly or indirectly to consumption), growth could still be increased by foreign aid so long as domestic savings do not decline by the full amount of foreign aid. But this raises the question of what happens to domestic savings after foreign aid declines or is terminated. Will domestic savings as a consequence of governmental policies remain lower than before foreign aid was introduced; be restored to their previous level; or increase as a consequence of the impact of growth on domestic savings via a positive marginal propensity to save?

Critics of the foreign aid pessimists, including Papanek and Dacy, accept the point that foreign aid cannot be regarded as a net addition to domestic savings as assumed by the earlier foreign aid models. However, they question the statistical methodology of the critics and point out that statistical correlation does not show causality.[21] Papanek concluded that a negative causal relationship between capital inflows and domestic savings is not supported by the statistical studies of the aid critics and that "only careful analysis of individual countries can really shed any light on the impact of foreign inflows on savings, exports or growth, and even such analyses are invariably subject to disagreement and dispute." He went on to say that there are no reliable answers to the question "What would have happened with less or more foreign resource inflows?" [22]

Dacy sought by means of a simulated analysis to derive some generalizations regarding the conditions under which post-aid growth rates can be higher or lower in comparison to a no-aid pattern of growth. He concludes that "a given amount of aid is more likely to stimulate the post-aid growth rate the higher the domestic savings ratio, the lower the percentage of aid tapped for government consumption, and the longer the term of aid." [23]

The theoretical and statistical debate over the relationship between foreign aid on the one hand and savings and growth on the other has continued in academic circles with the recent contribution of Paul Mosley entitled, "Aid, Savings and Growth Revisited." [24] Mosley examines some of the earlier studies mentioned above and provides his own disaggregated approach in which he explores the relationship between aid and growth for different categories of countries. He points out that one of the difficulties with the earlier statistical studies is that they lack a lag structure. A number of countries which have experienced high growth rates accompanied by high savings rates received large concessional aid flows during the 1960s (e.g., Korea and Taiwan), but continued to grow rapidly during the 1970s even though their concessional aid had by then become negligible. He finds substantial differences in the relationship between foreign aid and growth for the poorest countries. For example, the aid-growth relationship is significant and positive for UK-aided countries, but insignificant for French- and Scandanivian-aided countries.

We do not find much support in the literature for generalizations with respect to the relationship between the quantity of aid on the one hand and the savings rate and the growth rate on the other based on cross-section analysis covering a number of countries. Not only must we look at the experience of individual countries, but our hypotheses must be based on a microeconomic analysis of the impact of aid rather than on cross-sectional statistical support for macro growth models. From the standpoint of aid policy, past and prospective savings behavior of a country should play a role in aid allocation and in the policy conditions set forth in agreements between aid donors and recipients.

THE ROLE OF PRODUCTIVITY IN GROWTH

The increasing emphasis of modern growth theory on productivity has greatly undermined the capital-oriented growth models which attributed a substantial portion of increased growth to capital inputs, including capital flows from abroad. Research on and statistical analysis of the sources of growth in the US and certain other developed countries dates from the 1950s,[25] but adequate data have not been available for similar studies on developing countries. However, there is no reason to suppose that the share of growth attributable to productivity and technical progress is greatly different in developing countries than in developed countries.

Perhaps the best-known work on the sources of growth in the US (and in other developed countries) is that of Edward F. Denison. Denison finds that during the period 1929-1976, US (potential) national income grew at an average annual rate of 3.18 percent and that total factor productivity (output per unit of input) contributed 1.25 percentage points (or 39 percent), and capital inputs contributed 0.47 percentage points (or 14.8 percent) of the annual growth rate. For the 1948-1973 period, the average (potential) rate of growth in US national income was 3.87 percent, to which total factor productivity contributed 1.68 percentage points (or 43 percent), and capital inputs contributed 0.71 percentage points (or 18.3 percent).[26] For US national income per person potentially employed, the 1929-1976 average annual growth rate was 1.63 percent to which total factor productivity contributed 1.25 percentage points (or 77 percent), and capital inputs contributed 0.19 percentage points (or 15 percent). Other scholars, including Abramovitz and Solow, have found similar high shares of per capita income growth attributable to productivity.

The methodology of Denison and others used for attributing sources of growth to various factors has been a subject of some debate in the literature, but most economists who work in this field agree that a substantial portion of the growth rate must be attributed to productivity and technical progress.[27] Whether the role of capital inputs in the growth process in developing countries is substantially greater than the role of capital inputs in developed countries is a question on which we have little evidence. However, many development economists have assigned a major role to technological change in accounting for growth in developing countries. It may be argued that technical progress would not be possible without capital investment and, indeed, Solow's model is based on the embodiment of new technology in new capital equipment, so that the rate of productivity growth becomes in part at least a function of the rate of growth in capital inputs. But as Richard Nelson has pointed out,[28] there is a high degree of interdependence among the various sources of growth, including technology and the increase in human skills or human capital, and these interdependencies are not captured by statistical efforts to attribute portions of growth rates to individual factors. The same reasoning applies to capital-oriented growth models that attribute a large portion of growth to capital inputs alone.

If we were to assume that capital investment per se accounts for 20 percent of the growth rate, contribution of concessionary aid or Official Development Assistance (ODA) which constitutes only a small proportion of capital imports of the developing countries is greatly minimized. In 1978 net external financial receipts of the non-oil LDCs totaled $65.3 billion, of which ODA represented $22.8 billion, or 35 percent, with the remaining 65 percent coming from other sources.[29] Total net external receipts constituted about 5.1 percent of the GNP of these countries, and about 25 percent of their gross domestic investment (GDI).[30] ODA therefore constituted only 9 percent of the GDI of these countries. If we assume capital investment per se contributes 20 percent of the growth rate of these countries, ODA would account for only 0.1 percentage point of a 5 percent per annum growth rate, or increase that growth rate by only 0.1 percentage point if ODA were doubled.

ODA represented about 4.8 percent of the GNP and about 25 percent of the GDI of the low-income oil-importing countries in 1978.[31] Again, assuming that capital inputs are responsible for 20 percent of the growth rate, ODA would account for only 0.3 percentage points of a 5 percent annual growth rate of the low-income oil importers. The point we have been making is not that ODA makes a negligible contribution to growth, but that in terms of modern growth accounting the quantitative capital contribution of ODA to LDC growth may be small. It becomes necessary, therefore, to show that ODA has certain catalytic or other effects on aid recipients that make its impact much more than simply a quantitative addition to their national incomes. It should be mentioned, however, that in the case of the poorest or least-developed countries (LLDCs), ODA in 1978 constituted 8.7 percent of GNP and perhaps 40 to 50 percent of their GDI.[32]

THE FOREIGN EXCHANGE GAP APPROACH TO FOREIGN AID REQUIREMENTS

Although foreign aid constitutes only a small portion of the GNP of developing countries, aid finances over half of the current account deficits of low-income oil-importing LDCs and a significant portion of the

current account deficits of middle-income oil-importing
LDCs.[33] In recent years it has become customary to
project aid requirements on the basis of projected
current account deficits, less what might be expected
to be covered from nonconcessionary capital sources.
The current account deficits are projected by estimating
the level of imports and exports associated with a target
rate of growth.   This approach was follwed in President
McNamara's annual addresses to the Board of Governors
of the World Bank in 1978 and 1980, and with certain
variations this approach has also been employed by the
World Development Reports (WDR) for 1980 and 1981.
    The projections of ODA requirements over the 1980-
1990 period for low-income oil-importing LDCs given in
the World Economic Report 1981 are derived from projections of a number of variables relating to two scenarios,
the Low Case and the High Case.   The variables projected
for the two scenarios include export demand by the
OECD countries, nonconcessional capital imports, savings
effort, fuel conservation and certain other indicators
of LDC performance.   ODA is also projected on the
basis of past trends for the Low Case.   Without additional ODA, the rate of growth of GDP under the Low
Case is projected at 3 percent per annum, but under the
High Case assuming higher export demand, larger nonconcessional capital imports, and improved country performance over the Low Case, GDP growth rate would be 4.1
percent.   Under the High Case, imports of goods and non-
factor services are projected at $127 billion in 1990
and in the Low Case at $98 billion, for a difference of
approximately $30 billion.   It is argued, however, that
if under the Low Case ODA were increased from the projected $54 billion by an additional $30 billion in
1990 at current prices, the higher growth rate of 4.1
percent could be achieved.[34]   In other words, the additional ODA would enable the oil-importing low-income
countries to have the same volume of imports under the
Low Case as under the High Case.
    If the difference between the Low Case and the
High Case were solely a matter of nonconcessional aid
flows and export demand, but with the same economic
performance by the low-income countries, it is difficult
to understand how the additional ODA would raise the
growth rate from 3 percent to 4.1 percent.   On the
other hand, if the additional $30 billion in ODA served
to induce better performance by the low-income countries,
the projected rise in the growth rate would be more
credible.   Otherwise, such projections are simply an
application of the foreign exchange gap model with all
its inherent difficulties.
    It should be pointed out that such projections
involve assumptions regarding the capacity of developing
countries as a group to make adjustments in their
current account balances and, by implication, in their

aggregate savings rates and in their capacity to make
productive investments. Since the external resource
gap and the saving gap must necessarily be equal, such
projections must rely heavily on the extrapolation of
past trends with assumed allowances for adjustment.
The resource gaps to be filled by total capital imports
constitute only a small portion of aggregate GDP of all
oil-importing LDCs--3.7 percent in 1975-1978.[35] Small
shifts in resource allocations from the projections
over a 10-year period (1980-1990) could yield large
changes in "required" ODA in either direction. Estimating ODA requirements given the projected current
account deficits also involve highly speculative estimates of sources of nonconcessional loans and direct
investments. Nonconcessional sources of external capital are sensitive to internal domestic policies that
affect the assessments of commercial banks and other
foreign investors of political and economic risks.
This is perhaps especially important in the case of
the middle-income countries, many of which are quite
capable of increasing their commercial debt provided
they pursue policies that will give potential foreign
creditors confidence in their debt servicing capacity.
This could also apply to some of the low-income countries whose credit ratings have fallen very low as a
consequence of political and economic instability and
poor financial management.

Criticisms of the Foreign Exchange Gap Approaches

The importance of the foreign exchange constraint
on economic growth has been brought into question in
recent years by substantial increases in international
reserves of a number of oil-importing developing countries, some of which have not experienced satisfactory
growth rates in recent years. These countries include
Argentina, Peru, Uruguay and Jordan; even India's reserves have grown about five-fold since 1975 to a
total of some $12 billion in 1980. Countries with satis-
factory growth rates such as Columbia, Egypt, Korea,
Malaysia, Philippines and Thailand have all increased
their reserves several-fold during the 1970s, despite
the fact that most of them continue to receive substantial amounts of concessionary aid.

In a recent study entitled Economic Development
with Unlimited Supplies of Foreign Exchange, Henry J.
Bruton [36] pointed out the limitations of ample foreign
exchange availabilities for promoting development when
the foreign exchange comes from remittances of nationals
working abroad or from petroleum exports, rather than
from exports produced by the manufacturing and agricultural sectors of dynamic indigenous economies. These
so-called "unearned" foreign exchange flows not only

fail to develop the productive sectors of the domestic economy, but frequently create a number of economic and political problems. Foreign exchange per se does not remove the bottlenecks to development created by the lack of skills, absence of management project evaluation capabilities, and the overvalued exchange rates created by large foreign exchange receipts which make nearly all tradeable commodities cheaper to import than to produce at home.

Bruton's arguments regarding the limitations of foreign exchange availability and the possibility that large foreign exchange resources may prove counterproductive is well illustrated by the recent history of Nigeria. Nigeria's pre-oil economy was one of the most robust in Africa. Between 1950 and 1964 real GNP was growing at an average rate of 4.5 percent and agriculture was the leading sector. During this same period manufacturing as a percentage of GDP rose from 1 percent to 5 percent. However, after 1964 the value of oil exports increased enormously, from $189 million in 1964 to $25.5 billion in 1980, or to 23.4 percent of GNP. During that time non-oil exports declined in real terms by some 60 percent to only $654 million in 1980. During this same period the output of Nigeria's directly productive sectors, agriculture plus manufacturing, declined from 61 percent of GDP to 28 percent. Nigeria was a major exporter of palm and peanut oil in the early 1960s, but in 1980 Nigeria imported some 400,000 tons of edible oil and exports fell to zero.

In no small measure the decline in Nigeria's directly productive sectors was a consequence of the "over-valuation of its currency." As the supply of foreign exchange from oil exports rose, the domestic currency appreciated from $1.40 per naira in 1963 to $1.83 in 1980, while over the same period consumer prices rose 436 percent as against 162 percent in the US. This meant that the terms of trade of agricultural exports fell sharply on the world markets and the prices of imported foods and manufacturers declined relative to domestic costs of production. In terms of the output of directly productive industries, Nigeria has been severely damaged by the large influx of foreign exchange. Much of the oil-financed investment has been directed to public sector construction carried out by foreign companies with apparently little spillover effect on the development of skills in the indigenous economy.[37]

THE EMERGING EVIDENCE OF THE IMPORTANCE
OF GOVERNMENTAL POLICIES FOR GROWTH

Disillusionment with the capital-oriented foreign aid models of the early 1960s came with the failure of the development programs in many countries that were recipients of large amounts of aid from both the US and from other bilateral and international sources, and the growing evidence that having the right domestic policies constitutes an indispensable contributory factor to successful development. Most of the successful developers, including Korea, Brazil, Ivory Coast, Philippines, Thailand and Malaysia, have received substantial amounts of ODA, but so also have some of the less successful countries such as Argentina, India, Pakistan, Tanzania, Zambia and Zaire. Some of the moderately successful countries such as Indonesia and Mexico owe their success in part to the fact they have become substantial petroleum exporters.

Since it is not feasible or particularly productive to attempt to relate various economic policies adopted at different times to relative rates of growth among LDCs on a cross-section basis, research on the impact of economic policies on growth has necessarily taken the form of case studies of individual countries. In recent years efforts have been made to examine the impact of various governmental policies on some of the basic determinants of growth. These have included monetary and credit policies as they affect savings and the allocation of capital; import substitution policies that involve a high degree of import protection; exchange rate policies that affect export performance; price control policies in association with exchange rate policies that determine both the relationships among internal prices and between internal and external prices; and tax policies that have an impact on incentives for saving, investment and production in different economic sectors.

Monetary Policies and Savings

Monetary and credit policies in most developing countries have been employed to hold down interest rates in the face of inflation generated by excessive monetary expansion and large fiscal deficits. Ronald I. McKinnon and Edward S. Shaw have analyzed the effects of what they call "financial repression" in the form of excessive growth in the money supply and interest rate controls. They find that financial repression contributes to low savings as a consequence of negative real rates of interest and to the misallocation of investment arising from various forms of credit controls.[38] Liberalization of the financial markets is frequently accompanied by improved economic performance. The sharp rise in interest rates on deposits and loans by banking institutions in South Korea in 1965 was shown to have been responsible for a quadrupling of total private savings by 1971 and a comparable rise in investment, which was a key element in that country's rapid economic growth in the 1970s.[39] Similar results from monetary liberalization have been found in Taiwan and other countries.

Trade and Exchange Policies and Growth

Beginning in 1969 the National Bureau of Economic Research (NBER) inaugurated a comprehensive project on Foreign Trade Regimes and Economic Development under the joint direction of Professors Jagdish Bhagwati and Anne Krueger. The project included case studies of the following 10 countries, each of which resulted in a volume in the series, written by different authors: Brazil, Chile, Colombia, Egypt, Ghana, India, Israel, Phillippines, South Korea and Turkey. In addition to the 10 country volumes which appeared during the mid-1970s, two volumes were published analyzing the results of and implications of the case studies: Anne O. Krueger, Liberalization Attempts and Consequences (1978), and Jagdish Bhagwati, Anatomy and Consequence of Exchange Control Regimes (1978).[40] These studies cover foreign trade controls and foreign exchange regimes of the countries mentioned from 1950 through the early 1970s, during which period most of the countries studied shifted their trade and exchange policies. These studies provided a sound empirical basis for certain conclusions with respect to the impact of policy alterations on export growth and economic development.

Although there are substantial differences in the economic and political histories of the countries studied so that many factors affected their exports and development experience other than trade and exchange policies, two broad conclusions are strongly supported by the evidence. First, the movement from heavy import restrictions and overvalued exchange rates toward more open economies and equilibrium exchange rates was accompanied by a rise in the rate of growth of both exports and GNP. Second, countries that during the period failed to liberalize their trade and foreign exchange rate experienced slow economic growth or stagnation and poor export performance. The poor performance accompanying inward-oriented as contrasted with outward-oriented policies arose from price distortions that discouraged exports in favor of high-cost import substitution, increased costs due to delays and inefficiencies of the bureaucracy imposing controls stifled competition within the country, and reduced rates of savings and domestic investment. These general findings do not mean that the authors of the studies found that the best strategy for a developing country at all times is to abolish all trade controls and adopt floating exchange rates. Even the most successful country studies (e.g., South Korea) employed import substitution policies especially during the early 1950s, but abandoned these policies as opportunities for expansion of domestic output by means of import substitution were exhausted.

Bela Balassa also conducted country studies of the effect of outward-oriented as contrasted with inward-oriented development strategies. Balassa's studies show that outward-oriented policies, which include equilibrium exchange rates, import liberalization, and free internal markets, have contributed substantially to the growth of production and exports in such successful developing countries as Korea, Singapore, and Taiwan; while both exports and industrial development were impaired by inward-oriented development policies in Argentina, India, Uruguay and Chile (prior to that country's revolution in 1973).[41]

Outward-oriented economic policies tend to promote exports in contrast to inward-oriented policies that tend to emphasize import substitution through protection. However, Balassa makes a distinction between first stage and second stage import substitution, with the former regarded as being important for achieving a certain level of industrialization. This is well illustrated by the experience of high exporters such as Japan and Korea.[42] Although the relationship between exports and economic growth has been debated among economists for a number of years, the remarkable export performance in manufactured goods of the relatively fast-growing Newly Industrializing Countries (NICs) has led a number of economists to reexamine the hypothesis that export-oriented policies lead to better growth performance than policies favoring import substitution. In a paper entitled "Exports and Economic Growth: Further Evidence,"[43] Belassa investigates the relationship between exports and economic growth for 11 developing countries that already have an industrial base, namely, Argentina, Brazil, Chile, Colombia, India, Israel, Korea, Mexico, Singapore, Taiwan and Yugoslavia, for the period 1960-1973. Using a Spearman rank correlation coefficient and multiple regression in a cross-section analysis, Balassa found high correlations between various measures of export concentration such as export growth rates and export shares on the one hand, and output growth on the other.

A later article (August 1981) by William C. Tyler entitled "Growth and Export Expansion in Developing Countries,"[44] extended Balassa's 1978 study by analyzing the export and growth data for 55 middle-income developing countries in a cross-sectional study. The author's results are the same as Balassa's: a strong cross-country association between export performance and GNP growth. The author concludes that "this suggests that countries that neglect their export sectors through discriminatory economic policies are likely to have to settle for lower rates of economic growth as a result." (p. 129).

In another study, Bela Balassa examines policy responses to "external shock" for 12 middle-income LDCs.[45] He found that continued outward orientation in the Ivory Coast, Thailand and Tunisia led to increases in their export market shares; while the largest losses in market shares were experienced by Jamaica and Tanzania, where government intervention in the market mechanism in general and protectionist measures in particular were most far-reaching. Balassa also found that "increases in export market shares had favorable effects on the rate of economic growth, whereas reliance on import substitution had the opposite effect."[46]

A recent AID study found that the economic reforms initiated in 1977 by the new government of Sri Lanka, which included: (a) the unification and floating of the exchange rate; (b) the liberalization of import restrictions; (c) the removal of price controls on most commodities; and (d) interest rate reform, were accompanied by a substantial rise in annual rates of growth after 1977, more than twice the average rate of growth over the 1970-1977 period. Nearly all sectors shared in the rapid growth, and open unemployment was reduced from about 20 percent to about 15 percent.[47]

The Example of Chile

Chile is a country that has achieved substantial economic progress in recent years with relatively small amounts of ODA and only modest borrowings from the World Bank and the Inter-American Development Bank (IADB). Chile's present government came into power in 1973 with an inflation rate variously estimated up to 1000 percent, with industrial and agricultural output substantially reduced from the 1970 (pre-Allende) levels, and with exhausted foreign exchange reserves and its international debt payments in arrears. The new government sought to deal with these problems by shifting from the state intervention policies of the Allende government to reliance on the private sector. Price and import controls were virtually abolished and the currency's exchange rate depreciated in line with domestic inflation which has gradually been reduced by fiscal and monetary restraint. Output in agriculture, mining and industry recovered substantially in 1974 and GDP rose by 4 percent in that year following two years of negative growth. With the collapse of the world copper price in the second half of 1974, Chile's international reserves declined sharply in 1974 and the first half of 1975. The strategy of the government was to reduce budgetary allocations sharply and to increase taxes by introducing a value-added tax and increasing income tax rates. The prices of goods and services marketed by the public sector, including petroleum and food, were raised to world market levels and adjusted frequently in line with costs. Interest rates were also freed in the financial markets.

The result of these measures was a decline in the inflation rate during the second half of 1975 and a substantial balance of payments surplus in 1976. However, output and employment together with real GDP fell in 1975, but GDP recovered moderately in 1976 and unemployment declined from nearly 20 percent to 14 percent of the labor force.

Inflation declined from a rate of nearly 100 percent in 1976-1977 to only 8 percent between December 1980 and September 1981. Between 1977 and 1979 real GDP grew by over 8 percent annually while export earnings rose at an average annual rate of over 30 percent, with a substantial rise in the share of exports in the form of agricultural products and manufactures. The current account deficit was more than financed by private capital inflow, and official reserves rose by $1.9 billion over the two-year period. Real GDP grew by an estimated 6.5 percent in 1980 and unemployment was reduced to 8 percent by 1981.[48]

Chile provides an important case history of how a shift from inward-oriented and government intervention policies to outward-oriented policies, including the freeing of private markets for goods and capital, can reverse a country's economic performance from one of declining output and severe disequilibrium to impressive growth, relative price stability, and increased diversification of domestic output and exports. Moreover, this was accomplished with only small amounts of external public assistance. However, it should be pointed out that the Chilean economy is relatively advanced, with an estimated per capita income of about $1700 in 1979 current prices.

The Supply of Entrepreneurs

The empirical findings of a positive relationship between open economies and growth are supported by new evidence on the supply of entrepreneurship in developing countries. The development literature in the early post-World War II period placed substantial emphasis on the lack of entrepreneurship as a constraint on development, and economists and sociologists put forth a variety of explanations for this lack and suggested approaches to overcoming it.[49] However, the actual experience in LDCs in the post-war period shows that a lack of entrepreneurship has not been a serious barrier to economic development and that industry and agriculture have readily responded to economic opportunities created by a liberalization of governmental policies. In reviewing both the empirical evidence and the development literature, Nathaniel Leff finds that, while some entrepreneurship problems remain, "earlier theoretical concerns that the lack of entrepreneurship would prove a serious barrier for economic development have turned out to be much exaggerated."[50]

CONCLUSIONS ON THE EVOLUTION OF DEVELOPMENT THEORY AND FOREIGN AID

Development theory has made enormous advances over the past 30 years. The critics of the bankable loan project approach of the World Bank and of the Truman Point IV program (which employed technical assistance but little capital) were correct in viewing these approaches grossly inadequate for realizing the economic goals of the developing countries. What was required were development institutions with both abundant financial resources and technical capacity. Economists formulated capital-oriented growth models to justify large global aid programs, but failed to analyze the basic elements of development strategy and the role of domestic policy in development. The capital-oriented models of the mid-1960s, such as the Chenery-Strout two gap model, showed the volume of external capital flow required to achieve a target growth rate provided that domestic policies assured the attainment of certain key parameters in the model, e.g., the savings rate, the capital-output ratio, and the export growth rate. These relationships do not provide us with a development assistance theory unless the parameters are linked to the required policy instruments for achieving them. Further, the skill-limit constraint in the Chenery-Strout model, which is perhaps the essential characteristic of low-income stagnating countries, is a highly complex phenomenon and its relaxation is clearly not a simple function of foreign aid, including technical assistance.

In criticizing capital-oriented or foreign exchange gap models we are not saying that capital does not matter or that only policy or technical assistance or institution building matters in the growth process. They all matter, but their contribution to growth is to be found in an interdependent self-supporting package and the separate contributions of the individual components are difficult to identify or attribute. For example in the late 1950s following the war between North and South Korea foreign aid constituted the major source of Korea's capital formation, and according to Anne Krueger this would have been true even under the best conceivable policies.[51] Nevertheless, without reasonably good policies concessionary aid itself could not have assured productive investment or growth. Moreover, the continued flow of concessionary aid to Korea during the 1960s and early 1970s was only one in a combination of factors that brought Korea to the threshold of self-sustaining growth.

To conclude this discussion of the relative roles of external capital and domestic policies in development progress reflected in the literature on development, we quote from a 1977 article by Gustav Ranis (former Chief of the Bureau for Program and Policy Coordination of AID):

But perhaps the most important among the not so subtle changes in LDC policy attitudes is the growing recognition of what increased participation in the world economy, via trade, capital and technology imports, can and cannot do. Such participation can, of course, give a substantial assist to any development effort--it provides a system with additional options, resources and flexibility--but the basic issue of whether society's development goals will be attained is likely to be decided at home. If an effort is being made to alter the domestic parameters, foreign capital can, of course, be helpful in effecting the often painful transition; it can also--analogous to an ample natural-resource base--help enable the system to persevere on the old tracks a bit longer. Either way, the impact is marginal; there are strict limits on what the rest of the world can do to affect performance of the typical developing economy. After years of overselling the impact of foreign aid and foreign capital, everyone now has a healthier, more realistic view of the problems and limitations.[52]

NOTES

1 See "The Inter-American Bank," Federal Reserve Bulletin, June 1940, pp. 517-525, for a background and text of the Charter for an Inter-American Bank proposed by the Pan American Union in April 1940.

2 The Articles of Agreement for the International Bank for Reconstruction and Development did not define "less developed countries." Some of the early development loans made by the World Bank included countries such as Australia and South Africa that are regarded as developed countries today.

3 Articles of Agreement, Washington, DC: World Bank, Article 3, Section 4(2).

4 Measures for the Economic Development of Underdeveloped Countries, (Report by a Group of Experts Appointed by the Secretary General, New York: United Nations, 1951). The Group of Experts included a number

of leading development economists from the US and other countries.

5   For a brief history of the formulation of esti-mates of aggregate aid requirements for developing countries, see Raymond F. Mikesell, The Economics of Foreign Aid, Chicago: Aldine, 1968, pp. 77-82.

6   Rostow's original formulation appeared in "The Take-Off Into Self-Sustained Growth," Economic Journal, March 1956, pp. 25-48. It was further developed in his Stages of Economic Growth, Cambridge: Cambridge University Press, 1961.

7   For a criticism of Rostow's take-off period, see Walt W. Rostow, ed., The Economics of Take-Off Into Sustained Growth (Proceedings of a conference held by the International Economic Association), New York: St. Martin's Press, 1963.

8   See "International Aid for Developing Coun-tries," Review of Economics and Statistics, February 1961, pp. 107-138; and "Notes on the Theory of the Big Push," in Economic Development for Latin America, New York: St. Martin's Press, 1961; see also Max Millikan and W.W. Rostow, A Proposal: Key to Effective Foreign Policy, New York: Harper and Brothers, 1957.

9   See Albert O. Hirschman, The Strategy of Eco-nomic Development, New Haven: Yale University Press, 1958, Chapter III.

10   J. H. Adler, Absorptive Capacity: The Concept and Its Determinants, Washington, DC: The Brookings Institution, 1965.

11   United Nations World Economic Survey 1963, Vol-ume I. Trade and Development: Trends, Needs and Policies, New York: United Nations, 1964.

12   See Statement of George B. Woods to the Minis-terial Meeting, Development Assistance Committee, Orga-nization for Economic Cooperation and Development (Paris, July 22, 1965), published by the World Bank, Washington, DC, 1965.

13   1968 Review, Development Assistance Committee, Paris: OECD, December 1968, p. 31. The target was later changed to .7 percent of GNP to be devoted to Official Development Assistance (ODA).

14   The well known two-gap foreign aid model of Chenery and Strout was put forward in a paper entitled "Foreign Assistance and Economic Development," which

was originally prepared as an AID Discussion Paper (Office of Program Coordination, Washington, DC: US Department of State, 1965). It was later published under the same title in the American Economic Review, September 1966, pp. 679-723.

15 Thus $r = \dfrac{I/Y}{k}$ where r is the target rate of growth of output, Y; I is annual domestic investment; and k is the capital-output ratio.

16 For a discussion of this point, see Constantine Michalopoulos, "Production and Substitution in Two-Gap Models," The Journal of Development Studies, Vol. 11, No. 4, July 1975, pp. 343-356.

17 For a review of statistical studies relating savings rates to per capita incomes, see Raymond F. Mikesell and James E. Zinser, "The Nature of the Savings Function in Developing Countries: A Survey of the Theoretical and Empirical Literature," Journal of Economic Literature, March 1973, pp. 1-25. Hollis Chenery and Peter Eckstein found that the average saving rate for the entire Latin American region rose only slightly, from 16.3 percent in 1951 to 16.9 percent in 1964, although per capita GNP rose by nearly 50 percent. Chenery and Eckstein, "Development Alternatives for Latin America," Journal of Political Economy Supplement, July/August 1970, pp. 966-1006.

18 See, for example, K.B. Griffin and J.L. Enos, "Foreign Assistance Objectives and Consequences," Economic Development and Cultural Change, April 1970; K. B. Griffin, "Foreign Capital, Domestic Savings and Economic Development," Bulletin, Oxford University, Institute of Economics and Statistics, May 1970; Kaj Areskoug, External Borrowing: Its Role in Economic Development, New York: Praeger, 1979; and Thomas Weisskopf, "The Impact of Foreign Capital Inflow on Domestic Savings in Underdeveloped Countries," Journal of International Economics, February 1972.

19 Cross sectional studies of the relationship between capital inflow and domestic savings for a number of developing countries made by different scholars have yielded a wide variety of results. For example, Gupta concluded from his cross-section study of 50 developed countries that foreign capital inflows have virtually no effect on domestic savings in the less developed countries. (See K.L. Gupta, "Foreign Capital and Domestic Savings: A Test of Haavelmo's Hypothesis with Cross-Sectional Data: A Comment," Review of Economics and Statistics, May 1970, pp. 214-216.) However, a number of other studies show that capital in-

flows have a negative impact on savings. See Mikesell and Zinser, "The Nature of the Savings Function," op.cit., pp. 12-15.

[20] H.S. Houthakker, "On Some Determinants of Savings in Developed and Underdeveloped Countries," in E.A.G. Robinson (ed.), Problems in Economic Development, London: Macmillan, 1965.

[21] See G.F. Papanek, "The Effects of Aid and Other Resource Transfers on Savings and Growth in Less Developed Countries," Economic Journal, September 1972, pp. 934950; and D.C. Dacy, "Foreign Aid, Government Consumption, Savings and Growth in the Less-Developed Countries," Economic Journal, September 1975, pp. 548-561.

[22] Papanek, "The Effects of Aid," op.cit., pp. 934-950.

[23] Dacy, "Foreign Aid," op.cit., p. 560.

[24] Oxford Economic Bulletin, May 1980, pp. 79-95.

[25] See, for example, M. Abramovitz, Resource and Output Trends in the United States Since 1870, Occasional Paper No. 52 (New York: National Bureau of Economic Research, 1956); and R.M. Solow, "Technical Change in the Aggregate Production Function," Review of Economics and Statistics, August 1957, pp. 312-20.

[26] Edward F. Denison, Accounting for Slower Economic Growth: The United States in the 1970s, Washington, DC: Brookings Institution, 1979, p. 105.

[27] For a discussion of the attribution problem as related to sources of growth, see Everett E. Hagen, The Economics of Development, Homewood, IL: Irwin, 1980, Chapter 12.

[28] Nelson, "Aggregate Production Functions and Medium Range Growth Projections," American Economic Review, September 1964, pp. 575-606.

[29] DAC data. ODA excludes World Bank and IMF loans and loans from ordinary capital resources of the regional development banks.

[30] Based on 1980 Review, Report of the Development Assistance Committee, OECD, Paris, November 1980, Table IV-9, p. 87 and p. 76.

31 Ibid. If India is excluded from the low-income non-oil countries, the share of ODA in GNP is 7.2 percent, or about 35 percent of GDI.

32 1980 Review, op.cit., p. 89.

33 In 1980 ODA represented 63 percent of the current account deficits of the low-income oil-importing LDCs and 16 percent of the current account deficits of the middle-income oil-importing LDCs. World Development Report 1981, Washington, DC: World Bank, 1981, Table 5.1, p. 49.

34 This explanation of the rationale for the additional ODA requirements was provided by an official of the World Bank.

35 World Development Report 1982, op.cit., p. 12. In 1980 the current deficit of the low-income oil-importing LDCs was 4.5 percent and for the middle-income LDCs 5.0 percent (p. 49).

36 Research Memorandum No. 83, Center for Development Economics, Williams College, July 1981.

37 Much of the above material has been derived from an article by Peter Kilby entitled "What Oil Wealth Did to Nigeria," Wall Street Journal, November 25, 1981.

38 McKinnon, Money and Capital and Economic Development, Washington, DC: Brookings Institution, 1973; Shaw, Financial Deepening in Economic Development, New York: Oxford University Press, 1973; and McKinnon, "Financial Policies," in Policies for Industrial Progress in Developing Countries, John Cody, et. al., eds., New York: Oxford University Press for the World Bank, 1980, Chapter 3.

39 See Gilbert T. Brown, Korean Pricing Policies and Economic Development, Baltimore: Johns Hopkins University Press, 1973, Chapter 7.

40 All the volumes mentioned above were published by Ballinger Publishing Company, Cambridge, Massachusetts for NBER. These studies were financed under research contracts with the AID.

41 Balassa's studies are summarized in The Process of Industrial Development and Alternative Development Strategies, Essays in International Finance No. 141, International Finance Section, Princeton University, December 1980; see also, Bela Balassa, The Newly Industrializing Countries in the World Economy, Elmsford, NY: Pergamon Press, 1981.

[42] "Second stage import substitution" involves the replacement of domestic imports of intermediate goods and producer and consumer durables by domestic production. Balassa, Process of Industrial Development, ibid., pp. 5-9.

[43] Journal of Economic Development, June 1978, p. 181189. Balassa's findings support those in a study by M. Michaely, Journal of Economic Development, 1977, and a study by Michalopoulos and Jay in AID Discussion Paper No. 28, 1973.

[44] Journal of Development Economics, August 1981.

[45] The Policy Experience of 12 Less Developed Countries -- 1973-1978, World Bank Staff Working Paper No. 449, Washington, DC, April 1981.

[46] Ibid., pp. 34-5.

[47] Thomas A. Morrison and Louis Arreaga-Rodas, Economic Liberalization in Developing Countries, Some Some Lessons from Three Country Case Studies; Sri Lanka, Egypt and Sudan, AID Disccussion Paper No. 40, Washington, DC, September 1981.

[48] Much of the material above on Chile is taken from "Chile's Economic Recovery Reflects Emerging of Demand- and Supply-Oriented Policies," IMF Survey, Washington, DC: IMF, October 26, 1981, pp. 338-340.

[49] See, for example, Everett E. Hagen, The Economics of Development, op.cit., Chapter 11; and Hagen, On the Theory of Social Change: How Economic Growth Begins, Homewood, IL: Dorsey Press, 1962.

[50] Nathaniel H. Leff, "Entrepreneurship and Development: The Problem Revisited," Journal of Economic Literature, March 1979, pp. 46-64.

[51] Anne O. Krueger, The Development Role of the Foreign Sector and Aid, (Studies in the Modernization of the Republic of Korea: 1945-1975), Council of East Asian Studies, Cambridge: Harvard University Press, 1979, pp. 208-212.

[52] "Development Theory at Three-Quarters Century," Economic Development and Cultural Change, Vol. 25, Supplement, 1977, p. 269.

2
The Basic Human Needs Approach to Development and Foreign Aid

Concern for the high proportion of absolute poor[1] in the low income countries has been reflected in development or growth strategies for decades, but making basic human needs of the absolute poor the central objective of development and foreign aid policy and formulating a unique strategy or approach for realizing this objective are of recent origin. It is worth noting that the "basic human needs" (BHN) approach has been largely orchestrated by the World Bank and the DAC and by national government agencies such as AID, rather than by United Nations organizations such as UNCTAD or groups under the control of developing countries themselves.[2] Generally the developing nations prefer aid programs that involve minimum conditions and interference with national objectives and priorities imposed by the donor.

The purpose of this chapter is to review the economic literature on the BHN approach to foreign aid, with special reference to the relationship between the BHN objective and that of economic growth.

In defining and analyzing the BHN approach, it is difficult to understand how it differs from what development economists concerned with a broadly based development strategy and with reducing the degree of income inequality without seriously impairing incentives have been advocating for decades. The basic elements of the BHN approach consist of (a) greater emphasis on increasing agricultural output in the traditional rural sector; (b) the adoption of technologies that increase employment; (c) more equitable distribution of social programs between urban and rural sectors; and (d) an increase in education and training with special attention to opportunities for the poor. Proponents generally seek to avoid a welfare state based on large transfers of income and wealth and massive state control along the lines of the Chinese model. Interestingly enough, however, the poor country that has probably been most successful in dealing with basic human needs is China.

In a recent article, Danny Leipziger[3] states that the BHN approach is not a "unique strategy for development;" is not an "international welfare program;" and is not an "optimal" approach in the sense of the "maximization of either growth or broader benefits in the short- or near-term." "There are long-run benefits from a program involving broadened access to social services and improved income distribution through greater employment of the poor. There are also potential new costs, primarily in the medium term: reduced investments elsewhere; increased taxation, perhaps to finance increased (and recurrent) budgetary expenses; increased inflation if the supply of goods lags behind the creation of purchasing power; and reduced levels of national savings associated with a wide distribution of income. These tradeoffs need to be considered explicitly. They also require attention of donors who cannot offset some of the opportunity costs of the strategy aimed at satisfying basic needs."[4]

Although BHN is not an anti-growth approach, maximization of growth is clearly not the primary objective. It is not simply a welfare program because its objective is to increase employment and productivity in the poorest sectors of the economy. At the same time the BHN approach rejects the argument that the best way to deal with poverty is to maximize growth in the sense of giving priority to those projects with the highest marginal social productivity regardless of their effects on income distribution.

IS THERE A CONFLICT BETWEEN MEETING BASIC
NEEDS AND GROWTH?

In his presidential address to the American Economic Association in 1955, Simon Kuznets put forth the hypothesis that the early stages of development are accompanied by a substantial increase in income inequality which is reversed only at a relatvely advanced stage.[5] The Kuznets hypothesis, often referred to as the Kuznets curve, has been the subject of investigation by a number of economists, some of which will be reviewed in this study. Several statistical studies appear to confirm Kuznets' hypothesis in one degree or another, but most of the evidence is based on cross-country studies rather than time-series for individual countries. However, the important issues for the BHN approach are (a) whether a strategy of maximizing growth is consistent with the maximum reduction of absolute poverty and the meeting of basic human needs; (b) whether there are reasonable tradeoffs among development strategies for the maximization of the two objectives; or (c) whether the objective of reducing absolute poverty requires the virtual abandonment of the economic growth objective.

Statistical Studies of Growth, Inequality and Poverty

There have been a number of statistical studies on the relationship between growth and income distribution and between growth and poverty with wide differences in their findings. On the basis of a cross-section study of 43 developing countries, Irma Adelman and Cynthia Morris examined the relationship between the shares of income accruing to the poorest 60 percent of the households on the one hand, and various performance indicators on the other. The authors found that "for the longest part of the development process--corresponding to the transition from the state of development of Sub-Sahara Africa to that of the least Latin American countries--the primary impact of economic development on income distribution is, on the average, to decrease both the absolute and relative incomes of the poor....The absolute incomes of the poor begin to rise with development only when the nation moves well into the 'intermediate level' of development. Further, even here the improvement is not automatic -- the poorest segments of the population typically benefit from economic growth only when the government plays an important economic role and when widespread efforts are made to improve the human resource base."[6] Similar conclusions on the effects of growth on income distribution and poverty appear in the World Bank/Sussex volume, Redistribution with Growth (Chenery, et.al., eds., Oxford: Oxford University Press, 1974). The introduction to this volume states that "It is now clear that more than a decade of rapid growth in underdeveloped countries has been of little or no benefit to perhaps a third of their population." (p.iii)

More recent studies by Michael Crosswell[7] and Gary Fields[8] do not find a consistent tendency for income inequality to increase with growth. Time series data for individual countries show that income inequality has not increased with the growth of the per capita income for a number of countries. Gary Fields' investigation of the experience of 13 countries, for which data on changes in income distribution over time are available, shows that in seven countries (Argentina, Bangladesh, Brazil, El Salvador, Mexico, Philippines and Puerto Rico) income inequality rose as measured by the gini ratio, but declined in five countries (Costa Rica, Pakistan, Singapore, Sri Lanka, and Taiwan) and probably declined in India. Fields' conclusion is that there is no general relationship between changing inequality of income on the one hand, and either the initial level of GNP per capita or the rate of growth on the other.

Crosswell's study finds that poverty is mainly a function of poor countries with slow growth rates and not a function of the pattern of growth within countries. Where rapid growth has occurred, it has almost always resulted in a reduction of poverty, but growth rates have been generally low in poor countries. Crosswell points out that over 80 percent of the world's poor are in the low-income countries, that is, with per capita incomes in 1977 of $300 or less. About half the population in this group is poor, with the poverty line measured at $200 GDP per capita in 1977 uniform purchasing power dollars.[9] Countries with incomes above $450 per year in 1977 accounted for only 14 percent of the poor (i.e., with incomes under $200 IPC).[10]

An article by Ahluwalia, Carter and Chenery[11] seeks to determine the effects of growth on the proportion or the number of absolute poor in the LDCs, with the absolute poverty line being defined as per capita GNP of $200 IPC. According to this study the major features of global poverty are (a) almost 40 percent of the total population of all LDCs lives in absolute poverty; (b) the bulk of the poor are in the poorest countries-- South Asia, Indonesia and sub-Sahara Africa; and (c) the incidence of poverty is 60 percent or more in countries having the lowest GNP per capita. In order to estimate the effects of growth on absolute poverty to the year 2000 for individual countries and groups of countries, the authors formulate a Base Case projection using (a) World Bank projections of aggregate income and population growth; and (b) changes in the distribution of income by deciles compiled by Ahluwalia's estimate of the Kuznets curve.[12]

The authors conclude from their analysis that "The net effect of the population and income growth projections is a decline in absolute poverty of about 10 percent in the low- and middle-income groups of the LDCs and considerably more in the upper-income LDCs." In overall terms, they find that in the Base Case "The number of absolute poor in all developing countries (except for centrally planned economies) would be on the order of 600 million people in the year 2000 when allowance is made for countries omitted from our sample." This is a significant reduction in the incidence of world poverty from 50 percent of the LDC population in 1960 to 16 percent in the year 2000.

The authors then make an alternative projection on the basis of what they regard as feasible policies for (a) accelerating growth; (b) improving distribution; and (c) reducing population growth. By changing the assumptions based on the results of policies for improvement, they find that poverty in the year 2000 is considerably reduced by the alternative projections, but that "the elimination of absolute poverty by the year 2000 is not a credible policy objective. Even though the number of poor is reduced to a third of its present level, more than 200 million remain below the poverty line."13

The principal policy implications from their simulations are (1) the very poor countries can make more progress in reducing poverty by rapid growth without changing income distribution in accordance with the Kuznets curve than can a slow-growing country with more equitable distribution such as India; and (b) for middle-income countries which tend to have more rapid growth and less equal distribution "improved distribution is often more effective in reducing poverty than is accelerating growth." With regard to national and international policies they conclude that "international trade and aid policies have their main impact on growth and relatively little effect on internal distribution." Their optimum policy for reducing world poverty is a combination of aid and development strategy that would accelerate the growth of poor countries through a redistribution of aid in their favor, combined with internal policies that would provide a larger incremental share to the poor within countries. This approach would reduce total GNP of all developing countries by 5 percent in the year 2000 from the Base Case projection, but the per capita income of the bottom 40 percent would be 45 percent higher.14

As is noted below, other economists have arrived at different conclusions with respect to the role of redistribution efforts in reducing absolute poverty. In part these differences may be explained by differing goals, say, between reducing the incidence of poverty to some low percentage, e.g., 10 to 15 percent, and virtually eliminating poverty regardless of the consequences for overall growth.

Redistribution and Growth

Those economists who are convinced there is a fundamental conflict between historical growth patterns and the amelioration of poverty conclude that special strategies are required for meeting basic human needs in poor countries. However, approaches to the problem differ substantially.

What might be called the radical approach is represented by the writings of Irma Adelman and Paul Streeten.15 They not only reject what has been called the "trickle down" hypothesis, in which growth in the leading modern sectors can be counted on to spread to the traditional sectors of the economy where most of the poverty exists, but they reject the "redistribution with growth strategy" associated with Hollis Chenery16 and others who would give a greater emphasis to promoting the growth of the poorer sectors of the economy through a reallocation of investment and technical assistance.

Rather, these economists advocate a radical redistribution of assets, focusing primarily on land (even at
the cost of negative growth rates); a massive program
of education; and eventually a growth strategy based
on labor-intensive production.[17] This strategy of redistribution first and growth later is difficult to
understand both because a redistribution of wealth may
well create such political and economic disorganization
that the poor themselves will become victims of a
reduced output (such as occurred in Chile during the
Allende regime), and because there are neither internal
nor external resources for massive education over a
short period of time. This approach appears to be
more of a prescription for political revolution than a
viable development strategy.

Ahluwalia and Chenery analyze the results of alternative policies for distribution and growth by means
of simulations. They find that a strategy of investment
redistribution provides a more efficient alternative
to that based on consumption transfers. "If income in
the poorer groups is constrained by lack of physical
and human capital and access to infrastructure, then
reallocation of public resources can provide a powerful
mechanism for removing these constraints. The extent
of resource transfer involved--2 percent of GNP per
year for 25 years--is not small, but it should be
feasible in many countries. Most countries have substantially increased the percentage of GNP mobilized
through taxation, although much of the increase is
absorbed by higher government consumption. Some combination of increased resource mobilization and redirec-
tion of investment should make it possible to finance
the transfer. Since such a strategy is aimed at raising
production in low-income groups, the precise form of
the investment is of great importance. In our simulations we have assumed that opportunities for productive
investment exist, although at some cost in terms of lower
productivity and GNP. In practice, identifying such
projects may prove to be as much of a constraint on
this approach as the availability of resources."[18]

The annex to the volume Redistribution With Growth
contains short case studies of the growth-income distribution experience of six countries during the 1960-1970
period. Except for India (which has pursued a widely
advertised policy of reducing income inequality), each
of the countries--Cuba, Korea, Sri Lanka, Tanzania and
Taiwan--had favorable trends in income distribution.
In Cuba the rate of growth in GNP (in constant prices)
was low during the period, only 1.5 percent per year.
In Cuba, Tanzania and Sri Lanka income redistribution
was in large part the direct result of a conscious
governmental policy, while in Korea and Taiwan, which
have had the highest growth rates of most any developing country (9.4 percent and 10.0 percent GNP growth

respectively), the "improvements in income distribution, while welcomed after the event, have been largely the byproduct of policies aimed primarily at economic growth."[19]

Increasing Growth Through a Redirection
of Investment In Favor of the Poor

But is a development strategy that gives a high priority to basic human needs necessarily in conflict with the maximization of growth over time? Is it not possible that a shift in the allocation of investment and technology directed to increasing employment and productivity of the poorest sectors of the economy inhabited by half or more of the population will over time contribute more to the growth rate than industrial and infrastructure projects in modern urban sectors? In many countries a basic cause of mass poverty is to be found in market imperfections and price disparities in both commodities and credit, coupled with gross inequalities in the distribution of social services. Urban workers are often provided with highly subsidized public housing, health benefits, and education opportunities, while few social services are provided to rural sectors.

Theodore Schultz and others have argued that poor farmers respond quickly to price and other incentives and that they can be made more productive by the right kinds of technical assistance, the provision of inputs such as good seed and fertilizer at reasonable prices, and adequate credits. An expenditure of $100 million that increases agricultural output for a large section of a poor country may yield a much higher return in terms of the social product than a similar investment in a factory or modern highway between urban centers. Unless one believes that the marginal productivity of labor in the traditional rural sectors is zero--a proposition that has been shown by a number of empirical studies to be erroneous--a strategy for increasing employment and agricultural output may prove to be the most cost effective way of increasing overall economic growth.

In his December 1979 Nobel Lecture on "The Economics of Being Poor,"[20] Ted Schultz pointed out that world poverty is mainly a problem of the rural areas of poor countries and that the solution to world poverty lies in (a) the removal of economic distortions produced by governments that discriminate against agriculture in favor of the urban population; and (b) investing in human capital--skills and knowledge--in the rural poor. He emphasizes that the poor have the same basic incentives for hard work and betterment as the well off, given the opportunities and the knowledge to achieve economic gain through output and productivity. But in addition to the removal of the widespread discrimination against farmers in poor countries, there is a need to devote capital to investment in health, education and training, and in agricultural research. He suggests that such investments will yield high returns. For example, he states that investment in agricultural research in India has yielded a rate of return of 40 percent in terms of increased agricultural production. It is obvious that Schultz does not believe programs designed to reduce poverty are in conflict with the maximization of economic growth.

In a very penetrating essay entitled <u>Basic Human Needs: A Development Planning Approach</u>,[21] Michael Crosswell addresses the question of whether a BHN approach to development (and, inferentially, to foreign aid strategy) is in conflict with growth, or whether a BHN approach may actually contribute to economic growth. Crosswell first raises the question of whether rates of domestic saving and investment need actually decline with a BHN approach. He points out that increased consumption of the poor may in considerable measure be at the expense of the consumption of the non-poor rather than at the expense of the saving. This could occur if public expenditures were reallocated, at least at the margin, from the urban sectors to services for health, education and sanitation in the rural sectors. He further points out that a "substantial part of the current expenditures on health, education and improved diet" might properly be regarded as investment since they tend to increase the productivity of labor. Also, expenditures on housing, water and sanitation facilities in the poor areas "represent increases in the physical capital stock since these expenditures produce durable assets and services into the future."[22]

Suppose rates of domestic savings and investment as usually measured do decline under a BHN strategy. Crosswell argues that considering that developing countries are characterized by under-utilization of labor and misallocation of resources, "a BHN approach that aims at increasing the income of the poor by generating productive employment tends to use both labor and capital more effectively in sectors and processes more appropriate to the factor endowments of developing countries." In other words, growth is not simply a function of increased capital, but of "using existing supplies of labor, capital and land more effectively."[23] In his conclusion Crosswell makes the point that substantial growth in output and income is a necessary condition for meeting basic needs in most developing countries. "The BHN approach provides explicit criteria by which to evaluate alternative patterns of growth, according to their contributions to increased and more productive employment and to adequate production and supply of essential goods and services."[24]

By means of cross-section analysis, Norman Hicks regresses a measure of human resource development on the growth rate of per capita real GDP over the 1960-1977 period for 83 developing countries. His proxy for "human resource development" is either (1) life expectancy in 1960, or (2) adult literacy in 1960, or (3) some variation of either (1) or (2). Hicks finds a strong correlation between his proxies for human resource development and per capita real GDP. However, his analysis does not indicate the proper mix of human resource and investment in physical capital.[25]

Further support for the view that the development goal of providing basic needs is not necessarily in conflict with economic growth is provided in an article entitled "Basic Needs Fulfillment and Economic Growth" by David Wheeler.[26] Wheeler specifies and estimates a growth model in which national output and generalized measures of health, nutrition, and education along with other variables are related. Using data from 12 Asian countries, 23 African countries and 19 South American countries, the author obtains results supporting the hypothesis that changes in domestic welfare are strong contributors to changes in labor productivity. He finds that "the argument that economic growth and the basic welfare of the poor are separable in the short run does not seem to be consistent with the available data. It may, therefore, be helpful for advocates of rapid growth to adopt a relatively broad concept of investment in human capital when very poor countries are being considered. Conversely, those whose concern for equity include the physical quality of life as well as the distribution of money income may justifiably retain an interest in rapid output growth."[27]

Implications for Foreign Aid Strategy

The specific role of foreign aid in promoting the preconditions for growth in poor countries will be considered in Chapters 5 and 6. Foreign aid strategies for assuring the participation of the rural poor in the development process must be adapted to special conditions in each country. However, the idea popularized by some economists that general development efforts of aid agencies tend to leave the rural poor unaffected and that these agencies must somehow correct the bias against them cannot be sustained as having general applicability. The following quotation from the introduction to Rural Development[28] summarizes the findings of this comprehensive analysis of Korean agriculture in relation to that country's general development experience:

> There is at least one fundamental lesson in Korea's experience for other developing countries. In the 1970s, the focus of most international aid-giving

agencies has been on ways to assist the rural poor. To many aid-givers the obvious solution to this problem is to see that the assistance given is applied directly to the poorest segments of the farm population. The 'trickle down' effects of more general development efforts, it is argued, take too long to reach the poor, even when they are not diverted altogether to the rich. Korea, however, is a country where "trickle down" did work. In a relatively short period of time, rapid urban and industrial development did lead to marked improvements in rural living conditions.

A study of Korea's experience also suggests that direct efforts to help the rural poor may be difficult to achieve prior to a major and general development effort. In the 1940s and 1950s, with the notable exception of land reform, the Korean government's ability to implement rural development programs was extremely limited. It was not only that general development efforts brought with them an enhanced ability to build roads, establish fertilizer plants, and the like. A case can also be made that it was overall development that made it possible to improve the quality of the agricultural extension services and to provide the government with the capacity to implement programs, such as the New Community Movement, aimed directly at rural areas. Perhaps Korea would have found the trained personnel to implement these programs even in the absence of rapid general development, and perhaps the government would have acquired the will and the capacity to support the efforts of these personnel. But there are grounds for skepticism. A more plausible view is that experience implementing successful export-led industrial growth paid off over time in an increased will and ability to do something comparable for the rural sector.

CONCLUSION

Our conclusion from this survey of the literature on the basic needs approach to development is that there is no a priori reason for a conflict between the rate of growth of poor countries and the meeting of basic human needs and the reduction of absolute poverty. Much of the poverty of developing countries can be traced to unemployment or employment in very low productivity activities, and the bulk of the absolute poverty is in the poor, slow-growing countries. If half the population is either unemployed or employed in very low productivity activities, per capita growth is unlikely to be either rapid or sustained, so that the principal objective of development policy must be bringing a high proportion of the workforce into productive employment.

NOTES

1 Poverty has tended to be a relative matter so that in the US, for example, the poverty level for the present generation would have been considered a lower middle-class level a generation or two earlier. Abject or absolute poverty is defined in terms of standards of nutrition, housing, sanitation and health care that are below the levels required for avoidance of human suffering and for reasonable life expectancy.

2 The basic human needs approach first appeared at the 1976 World Employment Conference organized by the International Labour Office and later was the subject of documents issued by the World Bank, DAC and AID. See Michael Crosswell, Basic Human Needs: A Development Planning Approach, AID Discussion Paper No. 38, Washington, DC: US Department of State, October 1978.

3 Leipziger was formerly Deputy Director of the Policy Planning and Analysis Staff, US Department of State, and is currently with the World Bank.

4 Leipziger, "The Basic Needs Approach and North-South Relations," in The Challenge of the New International Economic Order, Edwin P. Reubens, ed., Boulder: Westview Press, 1981, Chapter 12.

5 American Economic Review, March 1955, pp. 1-28; see also, Simon Kuznets, "Quantitative Aspects of the Economic Growth of Nations, VIII: Distribution of Income by Size," Economic Development and Cultural Change, 11, No. 2, January 1963, Part II, pp. 1-80.

6 Irma Adelman, "Development Economics -- A Reassessment of Goals," in Papers and Proceedings, American Economic Review, May 1975, pp. 302-309; and Irma Adelman and C. T. Morris, Economic Growth and Social Equity in Developing Countries, Stanford: Stanford University Press, 1973, p. 81.

7 "Growth, Poverty Alleviation and Foreign Assistance," in Basic Needs and Development, Danny M. Leipziger, ed., Cambridge: Oelgeschlager, Gunn and Hain, 1981, Chapter 5.

8 Poverty, Inequality and Development, Cambridge: Cambridge University Press, 1981.

9 Uniform purchasing power dollars are calculated according to a formula designed by the United Nations International Comparison Project (IPC). For methodology, see Irving B. Kravis, et.al., "Real GDP Per Capita for More than 100 Countries," Economic Journal, June 1978, pp. 215-242.

10 IPC dollars are measured in dollars of 1970 US prices. Therefore, 200 IPC dollars is equivalent to $440 in 1980, or $474 in mid-1981 prices.

11 M.S. Ahluwalia, N.G. Carter and H.B. Chenery, "Growth and Poverty in Developing Countries," Journal of Development Economics, 6, 1979, pp. 299-341.

12 According to Ahluwalia's estimate "between the income levels of 200 and 800 IPC dollars the share of the lower 60 percent declines from 32 percent to 23 percent of national income. A country that followed this average relation would have about 80 percent of the increment of income accruing to the upper 40 percent of its citizens and quite modest increases for the remaining groups." See Ahluwalia, et.al., "Growth and Poverty," op.cit., pp. 308-9. Ahluwalia's original work was entitled "Inequality, Poverty and Development," Journal of Development Economics, September 1976, pp. 307-342.

13 Ahluwalia, et.al., "Growth and Poverty," op.cit., p. 329.

14 Ibid.

15 See Frances Stewart and Paul Streeten, "New Strategies for Development: Poverty, Income Distribution and Growth," Oxford Economic Papers, November 1976, pp. 381-405.

16 Hollis Chenery, et.al., Redistribution with Growth, Oxford: Oxford University Press, 1974.

17 Irma Adelman, "Development Economics--A Reassessment of Goals," op.cit., pp. 307-309.

18 Ahluwalia and Chenery, "A Model of Distribution and Growth," in Redistribution with Growth, op.cit., Chapter XI.

19 Chenery, et.al., "Redistribution with Growth: Some Country Experience," op.cit., pp. 253-290.

20 Theodore W. Schultz, "Nobel Lecture: The Economics of Being Poor," Journal of Political Economy, August 1980, pp. 639-651.

21   In Basic Human Needs, op.cit., Chapter 1.

22   Crosswell, Basic Human Needs, op.cit., pp. 21-22.

23   Ibid., p. 23.

24   Ibid., p. 24.

25   Norman Hicks, Economic Growth and Human Re-sources, World Bank Staff Working Paper No. 408, Washington, DC, July 1980, pp. 18-19 and 28.

26   Journal of Development Economics, July 1980, pp. 435-451.

27   Ibid., p. 450.

28   Rural Development: Studies in the Moderniza-tion of the Republic of Korea, 1945-1975, by Sung Hwan Ban, Pal Yong Moon, and Dwight H. Perkins, Cambridge: Council on East India Studies, Harvard University, 1980, p.10.

3
The Meaning and Significance of Concessionary Aid

Concessionary aid may be defined as any capital transfer the interest and repayment terms of which are less than those available to the recipient in the private market and is provided principally for noncommercial objectives. Some government-sponsored export credits carry terms that are more favorable to the borrower than those generally available in the private market. Here the primary purpose is to promote exports rather than to provide development assistance. Hence, US Export-Import Bank credits to developing countries often involve interest rates that are lower than those available in private financial markets, but are nevertheless not regarded as concessionary aid.

Concessionary aid for development is generally provided by governments or by multilateral public institutions such as the World Bank and the regional development banks. The terms on which concessionary aid is provided range all the way from outright grants and IDA loans that carry no interest with 50-year maturities, to World Bank loans that bear interest rates related to the Bank's cost of borrowing. Concessionary aid from governmental and multilateral public institutions is frequently referred to as official development assistance (ODA). However, ODA has not been defined uniformly in various official publications and is, therefore, subject to a certain amount of confusion. The OECD Development Assistance Committee (DAC) defines ODA to include disbursements of all types by donor countries, including both bilateral assistance and contributions to multilateral institutions, but not the disbursements by the multilateral institutions themselves.[1]

However, the World Development Report (WDR) employs the term ODA to cover grants and concessionary loans received by developing countries from both bilateral (including both DAC members and OPEC countries) and multilateral institution sources.[2] In this definition concessionary loans are restricted to those with a substan-

41

tial grant element. Unless otherwise indicated, we shall employ the WDR definition of ODA.

Although we have defined concessionary loans as those which provide more favorable terms than those available on the international financial markets, the DAC Reports exclude from concessionary loans all IBRD loans except Third Window loans (on which interest rates are subsidized), all International Finance Corporation (IFC) loans, all regional development bank loans from ordinary capital sources, and all IMF credits except those made by the IMF Trust Fund.[3] The general rule employed by the DAC is that for a loan to be regarded as concessionary, it must be intended to promote development and involve at least a 25 percent grant element.[4] Except for the loans from the IMF Trust Fund, IMF disbursements are not regarded as development assistance even though many of them involve a substantial grant element. Although the WDR does not define "concessionary" loans in its concept of ODA, we shall assume that it is identical with the DAC definition.

An important characteristic of concessionary aid, however defined, is that in nearly all cases it is provided under conditions that seek to influence the policies of the recipients and/or the allocation of their resources, and in many cases is combined with technical assistance. In the case of foreign development assistance with a relatively small grant element, this characteristic may be the most important distinction between concessionary and non-concessionary external capital inflow. Indeed we shall argue in a subsequent chapter that policy influence, project preparation and appraisal, and technical assistance for institution building and training are likely to constitute the most important component of the foreign aid package, particularly in the case of those countries that have not achieved the fundamental preconditions for self-sustained growth.

For the purposes of this study we shall include in concessionary aid all assistance from governments and government-sponsored multilateral institutions that involve a grant element, where the assistance is provided principally for noncommercial objectives. Nevertheless, we shall recognize the distinction between assistance characterized by a large grant element and loan assistance such as that provided by the World Bank involving a relatively low grant element and will discuss the rationale for the two types of assistance. We shall also distinguish between development assistance and the relatively short-term credits provided by the IMF under its normal credit facilities. However, as will be discussed in Chapter 5, the initiation of World Bank structural adjustment lending and the recent extended facility credits made available by the IMF have tended

to blur the distinction between development and balance
of payments assistance.

WORLD BANK, REGIONAL BANKS AND IDA LOANS

The grant element in an IDA loan is over 90 percent,
but that involved in World Bank loans may be only 10 or
15 percent. While rates of interest on World Bank,
IADB and Asian Development Bank (ADB) loans must in the
long-run cover the cost of the Banks' own borrowing in
the financial markets of the world, borrowers from
these institutions receive better terms than they would
if they borrowed directly from international financial
markets for two reasons. First, the Banks assume the
economic and political risks of default by the borrower;
and second, since the Banks borrow billions of dollars
each year in various national and world markets, they
are able to obtain better terms than an individual
borrower obtaining loans from international financial
markets. The Banks also arrange special loans from
governments of industrial countries or of OPEC countries,
often on better terms than those available in free
financial markets. (The Banks also have a certain
amount of funds from paid-in subscriptions on which
they pay no dividends.) Finally, some countries have
credit standings so low that they would be unable to
obtain the additional funds represented by their borrowings from the international development banks on
most any terms from the private financial markets.
Thus, the existence of these Banks increases the borrowing capacity of many of their members. In some
cases borrowing from the Banks actually increases the
ability of the member to expand its borrowing capacity
from the private international markets. This is accomplished by means of parallel loans and cross-default
arrangements which provide better security from default
for the private international lenders.

One further advantage of World Bank and regional
development bank loans over borrowing in private financial markets is that the maturities of the Banks'
loans are longer than those generally available to
countries borrowing in private financial markets.
Maturities of World Bank loans usually run from 15 to
20 years, including a grace period of four or five
years during which no repayments need to be made. This
tends to increase the borrowing capacity of Bank members
since by extending the period of repayment the debt-
service ratio is lower for a given amount of borrowing
than it would be in the case of borrowing, say, in the
Eurocurrency market where maturities run from three to
seven years.

Even though the World Bank and the regional development banks do not directly subsidize the borrower by

providing funds at rates less than the Banks themselves
can borrow, the additional borrowing by developing countries made possible by the operations of these institutions is not costless to the industrialized country
members that effectively guarantee the bonds of the
World Bank and of the regional institutions. The
increased demand for funds raises world interest rates
and absorbs capital that would otherwise have been
available to countries that do not borrow from these
institutions.

Criteria and Eligibility for World Bank, IDA and Regional Development Bank Loans

The World Bank has stated that its criteria for
World Bank loans is the same as that for IDA loans. By
loan criteria we mean the economic justification of the
projects and programs in terms of their direct and
indirect impact on the social product, the internal
rate of return on the investment that is assisted, and
the priority of the project or program in relation to
the develpment strategy of the country. The World Bank
and IDA as well as the regional development banks
finance economic programs for the agricultural and
industrial sectors, for infrastructure, and for social
programs in the areas of health, education, housing and
rural development that can be justified mainly in terms
of meeting basic human needs or other development
objectives not necessarily in direct support of growth
or the achievement of a condition of sustained growth.
Although it may be possible to show that programs designed to achieve social objectives also have a positive
impact on the rate of growth, the loans of the World
Bank, IDA and regional development banks, including
their soft-loan windows, need not be justified specifically on the basis of the contribution of the program
to economic growth. The loan criteria of these institutions encompasses a broad range of development objectives.

Within the framework of their loan criteria, the
World Bank, IDA and regional development banks maintain
eligibility rules for borrowing by member countries,
but eligibility appears to be somewhat flexible.
Eligibiliity for IDA loans includes both the least
developed countries--generally with per capita incomes
of under $370 (1979 dollars)--and the lower income
MICs with per capita incomes of between $371 and $680
(1979 dollars). About 90 percent of IDA's loan commitments in 1980 were to the least developed countries.

Eligibility for World Bank loans as well as loans
by regional development banks include all middle-income
countries, defined by the World Bank as those with per
capita GNP between $371 and $1,895 (1979 dollars), but
there have been World Bank loans to countries with

higher per capita incomes during the fiscal years 1980 and 1981, including loans to Portugal and Yugoslavia. The eligibility list continues to change and it will be remembered that Australia and Japan once received development loans from the Bank. Per capita income rather than the achievement of a condition of sustained growth constitutes the principal basis for eligibility.

The World Bank, IADB and ADB make loans to countries such as Argentina, Brazil, Colombia, Korea, Malaysia, Mexico, the Philippines, Portugal, Turkey and Yugoslavia, all of which have a well-established industrial base, substantial export earnings, and either a relatively high growth rate or the capability of achieving one. Actually, well over half the loans from the international development lending institutions (excluding IDA and soft-loan windows of regional lending institutions) go to the above-named countries. Some of these countries are included in the group which the OECD has called Newly Industrializing Countries (NICs), e.g., Brazil, Korea, Mexico, Portugal and Yugoslavia.

The countries listed in the previous paragraph receive the vast bulk of their external finance from nonconcessionary sources. In 1979 net capital imports from nonconcessionary sources constituted nearly 70 percent of the total net capital flows of middle-income countries (including the NICs). World Bank and regional development bank loans from ordinary capital resources provided only about 6 percent of the net external capital receipts of these countries in 1979.[5] Nevertheless, the contribution of the multilateral development banks to the economic growth of the middle-income countries is undoubtedly much larger than is indicated by the share of their net loans in the total net external capital receipts of these countries. Perhaps more important is the influence of the development banks on the development policies and strategies of these countries.

An interesting question which is perhaps beyond the terms of reference of this report is whether there should be more stringent eligibility requirements for borrowing from the World Bank and the regional development lending institutions and, if so, should the eligibility criteria be per capita income or growth rates, or some combination of the two? Clearly for countries that have achieved the capacity for self-sustained growth, foreign private loans and credits and foreign direct investment should be the principal channel for transferring technology, managerial talent and capital resources. For countries that have achieved a condition of self-sustained growth, but nevertheless have per capita incomes well below those of the industrialized countries, say, under $1,500 in 1980 dollars, a case can be made for permitting them to borrow from the World Bank and regional development banks in order to

46

increase their growth rates. For countries that are
both growing rapidly and will approach the per capita
incomes of the industrialized countries within the
next decade, serious consideration might be given to
restricting their access to the multilateral development
loan agencies.

The International Finance Corporation (IFC)

The IFC makes loans and equity investments in the
private sectors of developing countries. Although the
grant element in this financing tends to be low or
nonexistent, IFC financing can have a powerful catalytic
effect on the indigenous forces making for growth.
IFC loan and equity commitments of just over $800
million in fiscal 1981 are very small compared with
World Bank commitments of $8.8 billion, IDA commitments
of $3.5 billion, and combined IADB and ADB commitments
of about $3.5 billion in 1980. The IFC absorbs both
political and commercial risks in its financing, and
by means of joint loan and/or equity financing with
domestic and foreign private enterprise, it serves as
a catalyst by providing confidence to private investors
both through its economic appraisal of investment projects and as a form of protection against governmental
expropriation and contract violations. The IFC has
financed a wide variety of projects in the private
sectors of its members. For example, it made a loan
of under a half million dollars for food processing in
Somalia; provided loan and equity financing for a
leather company in Bangladesh; helped finance a coal
mining company in Zimbabwe; and a glass container
company in Jamaica -- all in fiscal 1981.

Depending upon the availability of private domestic
and foreign investment, greater use of IFC financing
might provide an alternative to financing wholly government owned and operated industrial enterprises in
developing countries, which in many if not most cases
have not proved to be as efficient as private enterprise,
and which do not mobilize private savings and entrepre-
neurial talent. The question of channeling more aid
to the private sector will be considered in a subsequent section of this Chapter.

IMF Concessionary Aid

Although IMF credits are regarded as balance of
payments rather than development assistance -- a distinction that will be examined in Chapter 5 -- it should
be recognized the IMF credits involve a substantial
grant element. The terms of IMF concessionary credits
range from the ten-year Trust Fund credits at 1/2 of 1
percent and repayment in semi-annual installments
beginning with the sixth year, to drawings under the

regular credit tranches and the Extended Fund Facility (with repayment over 10 years at 6 1/4 percent in 1981).[6] Loans from the Trust Fund are made only to low-income countries, but credits under the Extended Fund Facility for dealing with "structural balance of payments maladjustments" are available to all developing countries and have been made to relatively high-income LDCs such as Mexico and the Philippines. In addition, credits under the Supplementary Financing Facility are made available under terms sufficient to cover cost of the Fund's borrowing from individual members, except for subsidized terms to low-income members.

THE IMPORTANCE OF THE GRANT ELEMENT IN CONCESSIONARY AID

As has been noted, the grant element in development aid may vary substantially from 100 percent in the case of grants to no more than 10 to 15 percent in the case of World Bank loans. Assuming that the nonfinancial contributions of the donor agency is the same for both loans, as is generally the case for World Bank and IDA loans, the difference in the financial contributions of the two types of loans is the difference between the present values of the principal and interest payments (if any) that must be made on the two loans. Thus the resources saved by receiving an IDA loan rather than a World Bank loan may represent as much as three-fourths of the face value of the loan. The contribution of the resources saved by a country receiving an IDA loan as contrasted with a World Bank loan will depend upon the overall economic policies and investment opportunities in the country.

The ability to obtain an IDA loan may enable the country to obtain resources from abroad that would not otherwise be available since the country might not be eligible for World Bank loans or other sources of financing with a lower grant element. In this case the contribution of the IDA loan to development would be much greater than that represented by the grant element alone, since the country gains the advantages of the involvement of a development assistance institution in its development program.

THE ALLOCATION OF ODA

ODA receipts by developing countries, whether under the WDR definition or the DAC definition as applied to receipts, cover bilateral and multilateral assistance with a grant element of at least 25 percent. Hence, ODA excludes World Bank and regional bank ordinary capital loans as well as certain bilateral loans. ODA is, therefore, used by DAC, World Bank and other official reports to identify "concessionary" as contrasted with nonconcessionary aid according to the DAC definition of concessionary aid given above. The allocation of ODA among different groups of developing countries classified by their per capita incomes has been a matter of considerable interest to development economists and public agencies. The issue is of special importance today given the fact that ODA is in short supply relative to other sources of external capital.

Although the non-oil low-income LDCs (defined by the DAC as having 1978 per capita GNP under $450) have been receiving nearly 60 percent of the total ODA receipts of the non-oil developing countries, per capita ODA receipts have been lower for these countries ($10 in 1978) than for the middle-income countries ($21 in 1978).[7] Per capita ODA receipts for the low-income countries as defined by the IBRD (1978 per capita GNP under $300) was nearly $16 in 1976. Michael Crosswell provides estimates to show that for the 1976-1978 period the group of countries that accounts for 80 percent of the developing world's poor (defined as 1977 per capita GNP under $300) received only 44 percent of ODA commitments, while countries accounting for less than 10 percent of the poor (1977 per capital GNP over $450) received 36 percent of ODA commitments.[8] This pattern of allocation can be explained in part by political and economic factors influencing preferences of bilateral donors. Analysis of the data by Crosswell and others show a bias against populous countries in terms of ODA per capita, and these countries tend to have the lowest incomes and the bulk of the absolute poor.

The DAC Reports and a number of development economists have expressed dissatisfaction with this allocation of concessionary aid and have argued for shifting ODA allocations so that per capita assistance declines as per capita income increases. One argument for allocating concessionary aid in inverse relation to the per capita incomes of the recipients is based on the expressed objective of giving primary emphasis to alleviating poverty. This is consistent with the basic human needs approach discussed in Chapter 2. If one accepts the argument also discussed in Chapter 2 that progress toward the alleviation of poverty is mainly a function of the growth rate in the poorest countries (which countries contain the bulk of the absolute poor), then ODA allocation on the basis of per capita income is not necessarily inconsistent with the objective of employing external assistance to promote growth. Another argument which might be called the international equity argument is that foreign aid should be allocated in such a way as to raise the average income of the low-income countries in order to reduce international disparities in per capita incomes without necessarily being concerned with the distribution of income within countries. A third argument which applies particularly to ODA is that low-income countries are often unable to meet the creditworthiness standards of the World Bank or of the private international financial institutions, and since ODA is more scarce than other sources of external capital, it should be allocated in favor of those countries lacking alternative sources of capital.

The argument against allocating ODA in inverse relation to per capita income is that aid allocation should be determined on the basis of its maximum contribution to growth, and that since countries with higher per capita incomes have more of the preconditions for growth, ODA can be more effective for growth inducement in these countries. It is true that it is easier to generate projects suitable for aid support in the more advanced LDCs, and this probably helps to explain the existing per capita ODA bias in favor of the higher income countries. On the other hand, establishing the preconditions for growth should be an important function of ODA and in the longer run might prove more effective in terms of the number of poor people whose incomes are raised when allocated to promote the preconditions for growth in the more populous countries. Presumably aid should be directed at helping the largest number of poor people regardless of their nationality rather than national states. However, a substantial proportion of bilateral aid is directed toward particular countries in support of the foreign policy interests of the donors.

A fundamental question in aid allocation is the performance of the recipient country, including willingness to adopt the appropriate policies required for growth. Allocating ODA simply on the basis of per capita income would constitute poor development assistance policy. We are, therefore inclined to agree with Crosswell[9] that both per capita income and performance, including policy, should guide the allocation of ODA, and that because of its scarcity it should be heavily allocated toward establishing the preconditions for growth in low-income countries that lack alternative sources of external capital.

CONCESSIONARY AID AND THE PRIVATE SECTOR

A frequently expressed criticism of concessionary aid is that the vast bulk of it flows to the public sector and that it has encouraged governments to operate in areas where private domestic or foreign enterprise could function more efficiently. There are two parts to this criticism that require separate investigation. First is the degree to which multilateral and bilateral development institutions have encouraged governments to operate in such industries as steel, construction materials, chemicals, fertilizers, plantation agriculture, petroleum, and mining and metallurgy that might have otherwise been left to the private sector. (We may exclude public utilities and transportation since not only are they universally regulated by governments, but in few countries, developed or developing, do they remain in the private sector.) The second is whether the industries operated by governments function less efficiently than they would if they were in the private sector.

Beginning with the first issue, we find no evidence that the availability of concessionary aid to government enterprise has influenced the creation or maintenance of the existing industrial ownership structure in developing countries. Most of the basic industries owned and controlled by government enterprises were initiated at a time when no indigenous capital and entrepreneurship was available to establish them, or the industries were foreign-owned and were expropriated by the government, usually for political reasons. There are some exceptions where governments have nationalized domestic industries or have gone into competition with them, but again it would be difficult to find cases where such actions were induced by the availability of concessionary aid.

The second issue relating to the relative efficiency of public vs. private enterprise is in part a matter of economic philosophy. However, we believe there is substantial evidence in favor of private enterprise, especially when it is not heavily regulated and is permitted to operate in response to market forces with respect to pricing, marketing (including exporting), product mix, and investment (including the existence of free entry into the industry by both domestic and foreign enterprise). Although it is possible to formulate models of government decision making that would approximate Pareto optimality conditions that would exist in perfectly competitive markets with perfect knowledge among the competitors, we are highly skeptical of their realism or feasibility. There are just too many political constraints on government enterprise to enable them to operate on the basis of full economic rationality. Losses by government enterprises have contributed notoriously to the budgetary deficits of LDCs, and dependence on government for investment budgets rather than on capital markets has often left them undercapitalized. In the mining industry, government operations have been shown to be substantially less profitable than private mining firms, after taking account of the fact that government enterprises are subject to lower taxation and capital costs than privately-owned mines. Moreover, few government mining operations have been able to create a large successful mining complex starting from grass roots exploration. Most large government-owned mines were explored and constructed by private enterprise.

In the field of agriculture, state-owned farms have had an almost universally poor record and the audits of World Bank loans to such enterprises that we have reviewed generally bear this out. Finally for those countries that have been successful in expanding their exports of manufacturers, the dynamic elements contributing to this success are found almost entirely in the private sector.

Although we reject the general criticism that concessionary aid institutions are responsible for the existing ownership patterns in the economies of developing countries, we support the view that these institutions should give greater emphasis to the stimulation of private economic activity wherever that is possible within the economic and legal framework of a developing country. These efforts should, of course, include the development of the domestic capital market as a source of equity and loan funds for the private sector. In their requests for concessionary aid, governments almost inevitably favor investment in the public sector so that it should be the responsibility of development institutions to find ways of stimulating private economic activity, whether in industry or agriculture. The reason is that the potentially dynamic indigenous forces for productivity and output growth are found in the private sector rather than in government bureaucracies and public sector projects.

Multilateral institutions such as the World Bank are constrained by their charters from denying loans to countries simply because they have centrally planned economies or state ownership of productive facilities. On the other hand, the World Bank is under no obligation to make loans for use by government enterprises that are grossly inefficient and unproductive, or are characterized by continual financial losses as a consequence of improper pricing policies.

If the US government were to adopt the position that socialist countries that allow no significant free enterprise activity are incapable of achieving a condition of self-sustained growth, the US might be placed in an awkward position politically. Should the US vote against every World Bank loan to China, Mozambique and Romania (as well as to any other Soviet Bloc states that may become members of the World Bank) on grounds that such loans simply support an economic system that can never achieve self-sustained growth?[10]

We are not prepared to answer this question, in part because of its political implications and in part because there is considerable evidence that it is possible for a country to achieve sustained growth within some form of socialist model (e.g., Romania and Yugoslavia).

We say this despite the overwhelming evidence that
private enterprise, free market countries are the most
successful achievers.

An Expanded Role for the IFC

One approach to channeling more external capital
to the private sector would be to increase the resources
and scope of activities of the IFC. This would undoubtedly require both imaginative innovations and some
departure from the IFC's current practices. For example,
the IFC might make larger equity commitments in both
domestic and foreign firms in order to initiate investment.[11] It might move vigorously into the financing and
organization of private development finance corporations
(DFCs) which would operate in both the industrial and
agricultural sectors. Joint financing packages with
the World Bank might be formulated which would provide
an incentive to a government to create greater opportunities for domestic and foreign private investment
in certain sectors. Undoubtedly the IFC staff has
prepared a number of imaginative proposals for expanding its activities with which the agency might be
willing to experiment given the encouragement and the
resources to do so.

Giving the IFC power to make concessionary loans
would not appear to be appropriate in the private
sector. One of the obstacles to the creation of efficient capital markets in developing countries has been
the tendency of governments to hold interest rates below
free market levels, and the IFC should not give any encouragement to this policy. On the other hand, the ac-
ceptance of greater risks for investing in projects that
contribute to growth is clearly in line with free enterprise practice and tradition.

NOTES

[1] DAC also uses the term ODA to identify receipts
of concessionary aid by developing countries, but the
statistical relationship between the two uses of ODA is
not known to the author.

[2] For a discussion of these definitions see World
Development Report 1981, op.cit., p. 55.

[3] See 1980 Review, DAC, op.cit., p. 209.

[4] The grant element is defined as the excess of a
loan's face value over the sum of the present values of
the repayments of principal and interest, discounted at
10 percent. See 1980 Review, DAC, ibid., p. 241.

5 1981 Review, Development Assistance Committee, Paris: OECD, 1981, Table IV-2.

6 Annual Report 1981, Washington, DC: IMF, p. 129.

7 1980 Review, DAC, op.cit., Table IV-IX, p. 87.

8 Reference is to Crosswell's "Growth, Poverty Alleviation and Foreign Assistance," AID Discussion Paper No. 39, August 1981. This is a revised version of an earlier article with the same title in Leipziger (ed.), Basic Needs and Development.

9 Crosswell, "Growth, Poverty Alleviation," op.cit.

10 Even if some of these countries were to adopt the Yugoslavian brand of socialism in which enterprises are permitted to engage in market activities, they could scarcely be regarded as free enterprise economies since capital cannot flow freely in response to profitability. The shares in Yugoslavian worker-owned enterprises are not transferrable and the state controls entry into industries. For a discussion of this issue see Milton Friedman, Market Mechanisms and Central Economic Planning, Washington, DC: American Enterprise Institute, 1981.

11 Currently the IFC's equity and loan commitments to individual projects tend to be a small proportion of the total investment in the projects.

4
The Condition
of Self-Sustaining Growth

In defining the condition of self-sustaining growth, we are not concerned with a variety of development goals, such as are included in the BHN approach to development. By growth we mean the average annual rate of growth in output per capita over time. Growth sustainability implies two conditions. One is the economic and social <u>capacity</u> of a country to grow on a sustained basis, or what has been referred to as the preconditions for growth. A country in which ninetenths of the population is rural might achieve for a time a per capita GNP rate of, say, 1 percent per year on the basis of coffee exports and a limited amount of import-substituting industrial output, while nonexport agriculture is poor and stagnating and there are no industrial exports. In such a country the growth base is narrow and even a low growth rate is unsustainable over time. For that country to achieve the capacity for sustained per capita growth of, say, 2 or 3 percent, there must exist the conditions for a sustained rise in the productivity of the agricultural sector, an expansion and diversification of the industrial base, and an expansion of the export base, including industrial exports. This is not to say that all economic sectors must grow at the same rate, but a country in which the productivity of the vast bulk of the population is low and stagnating and lacks the institutions for economic progress has not achieved the preconditions for sustained growth.

A second condition of growth sustainability has to do with the governmental policies and the commitment on the part of its leaders to growth. Countries with the capacity or preconditions for growth may not have a record of sustained growth regardless of the amount of external assistance they receive. Likewise, countries may not be making progress in achieving the preconditions for sustained growth in the absence of appropriate policies and a commitment to development, again regardless of the availability of external assistance.

The concept of <u>self</u>-sustained growth implies the

ability of a country to maintain an acceptable rate of growth on a sustained basis in the absence of concessionary aid. Such countries should be able to maintain their growth rates with the aid of external capital obtained from nonconcessionary sources. Although loans from concessionary sources such as the World Bank might enable them to increase their external resource flow, concessionary aid is not required to maintain acceptable rates of growth.

The concept of self-sustained growth implies that sustained growth can be achieved for a time with concessionary assistance, but not necessarily without it. It might also mean that without concessionary aid growth could be maintained but only at a very low rate. In defining the concept of self-sustained growth it should be emphasized that we are not suggesting that concessionary assistance can sustain growth without appropriate governmental policies and development programs and priorities, or that external financial assistance alone can create the preconditions for sustained growth. Concessionary aid is development assistance, including not only capital but project and program formulation and appraisal, and frequently includes a technical assistance component. The exact nature of the development assistance package depends on the conditions in each recipient country.

The above definition of self-sustained growth does not provide a standard or minimum rate of growth or a minimum per capita income base. All that is implied is that the per capita growth rate be positive. However, as a meaningful goal for foreign aid administration we require some quantitative standard since, for example, self-sustained growth in per capita GNP of less than 1/2 of 1 percent per year would not have much significance. We shall arbitrarily define economic growth on a self-sustained basis as an annual rate of increase in per capita GNP of at least 2.5 percent, which can reasonably be expected to be maintained without concessionary aid.

A case can be made for supplementing the growth rate criterion with a minimum per capita income. First, the historical pattern of growth shows that a reasonably well diversified economy--which is probably necessary for sustained growth--is not achieved until a certain level of per capita income is reached. Second, very few countries have achieved an average annual rate of per capita growth of 2.5 percent over a 10-year period with annual per capita incomes of less than $600 in 1979 dollars, which is approximately $200 above the IBRD cutoff point between low-income and middle-income LDCs.[1] Moreover, the countries that have maintained satisfactory growth rates with per capita incomes of under $1000 have been heavily dependent on concessionary aid. Third, very poor countries must achieve per capita

growth rates substantially higher than 2.5 percent if
they are to make reasonable progress toward eliminating
absolute poverty for the lowest 40 percent of the income
receivers. Hence, they should not be denied concessionary aid even if their growth rate exceeds the minimum
standard. Given the typical income distribution of
developing countries in which the lowest 40 percent of
the income receivers receive 10 to 15 percent of the
total income, a critical average per capita income is
necessary in order to raise that 40 percent of the
population above the level of absolute poverty. If we
establish the level of absolute poverty at only $200
per year in 1980 dollars, it would require an average
per capita income of $600 to $800 to provide the lowest
40 percent of the income receivers with $200 per year.
We might be justified therefore in establishing the
additional criterion of a minimum per capita income of
$1000 in 1980 dollars in defining economic growth on a
self-sustaining basis.

In establishing the criteria for a condition of
self-sustaining growth we are not determining eligibility for ODA or concessionary aid as defined by the
DAC. We have already discussed reasons for suggesting
that ODA should go only to the poorer countries, and
that higher income LDCs should not be eligible for ODA
simply because they have not achieved a sustained per
capita GNP growth rate of 2.5 percent per annum. The
higher a country's per capita GNP and the more diversified its economic base, the less likely ODA can be
justified for helping a country achieve a satisfactory
growth rate. ODA is both a scarce and a highly subsidized capital resource and should be made available
only to the poorest countries. This principle is, of
course, recognized in the eligibility of countries for
IDA loans. By and large, middle-income LDCs should be
expected to obtain their development assistance on
terms comparable to those for the World Bank loans.

LEVELS OF PROGRESS TOWARD THE CONDITION OF
SELF-SUSTAINING GROWTH

There exists a broad spectrum of progress toward
the condition of self-sustaining growth among developing
countries. Moreover, each LDC is unique in terms of
the combination of positive and negative economic,
social, institutional and political factors that affect
progress toward self-sustaining growth. Therefore, we
shall not attempt to group all developing countries by
stage of progress in terms of a limited set of quantifi-
able standards. Nevertheless, in presenting the following broad categories of countries we shall suggest
examples of countries that are illustrative of each
stage. In presenting these categories in broad non-

quantitative terms, we are particularly interested in
identifying the unique role of concessionary aid in
assisting countries in each stage. This broad framework
will be employed in the following chapter in analyzing
the effectiveness of concessionary aid in promoting
self-generating growth.

We list the following stages of progress toward
self-sustained growth beginning at the bottom of the
scale:

1. Countries which are grossly deficient in the
preconditions for growth and which have a per capita
GNP of under $300 in 1980 dollars.

Many of the countries of sub-Saharan Africa that
are just emerging from a primitive tribal status and in
which the vast bulk of the population is illiterate are
illustrative of this stage. For such countries ODA-
type assistance can be quite effective in promoting the
preconditions for growth, but should be accompanied by
substantial involvement in the development process by
the aid agency, including technical assistance packages
designed to reach a high proportion of the productive
agents, especially farmers.

Concessionary aid to such countries should depend
upon the existence of reasonably adequate policies and
a commitment on the part of the leaders to development.
Where such conditions do not exist there are likely to
be few projects for promoting the conditions for sustained growth that would meet the test of aid effectiveness. Ghana might be illustrative of this subcategory.
In the absence of appropriate policies, financing infrastructure projects such as roads, or program financing for industrial or agricultural imports are likely
to encourage governments to persist in policies anti-
thetical to growth. On the other hand, a dialogue
between development assistance agency personnel and the
government should be maintained with the hope of influencing a change in government policies which would
make possible the formulation and implementation of aid-
supported projects which have a reasonable chance of
success in contributing to growth. (There are, of
course, countries such as Chad, Ethiopia and Uganda
where political conditions have deteriorated to the
point at which even a useful dialogue with a development
assistance agency may be impossible.)

2. Countries which are lacking many of the institutional and other preconditions for sustained growth,
but where there exists a core of technically trained
personnel, where adult literacy is in the range of 20-
40 percent, where there is considerable infrastructure
and import substituting industry, and some progress has

been made in raising agricultural output through the
introduction of modern technology.

The countries of the Indian subcontinent and Sri
Lanka are illustrative of this stage. The countries
in this category account for the largest share of
total population of LDCs and also for the bulk of the
Third World's absolute poor. A large proportion of
the available ODA might be usefully concentrated in
these countries and aid should be accompanied by a
substantial component of development guidance and technical assistance.

3. Middle-income countries that have acquired
most of the preconditions for self-sustained growth but
are unable to obtain on nonconcessionary terms sufficient external capital to achieve or maintain a per
capita growth rate of 2.5 percent.

Some of these countries have been following reasonably good policies and have a record of steady progress
toward self-sustained growth for more than a decade
with the help of concessionary aid. This subcategory
might be illustrated by Colombia, Ivory Coast and
Thailand. In accordance with present IDA standards
most of the countries in this group are ineligible for
ODA, but they should continue to be eligible for loans
from the World Bank and the ordinary capital loans of
IADB and ADB. However, there are some countries in
this category that are not making satisfactory progress,
largely as a consequence of poor policies. Boliva and
Honduras might be illustrative of this subcategory. In
the case of these countries a dialogue with development
agencies should be maintained, but any development
assistance should be limited to World Bank-type loans
and made available only as the governmental climate for
development shows signs of improvement.

4. Relatively advanced countries with reasonably
good institutional structures and human resources base
for self-sustained growth and with per capita GNP above
$1000 in 1980 dollars.

Some of these countries, such as Brazil, Mexico,
and Korea, have been making rapid economic progress,
but continue to receive concessionary aid for a marginal
portion of their capital imports. A case can be made
for limiting concessionary aid to countries at this
stage only in exceptional circumstances, such as a
situation in which their growth is aborted by external
shocks. Clearly the World Bank Articles of Agreement
(Art. III, Sec. 4) requirement that the borrower is
otherwise unable to obtain the loan on reasonable terms,
has particular relevance for this category of country.

There is a subcategory of this group of countries that are growing slowly or stagnating as a consequence of inappropriate governmental policies, and in addition have serious external debt problems that restrict access to nonconcessionary loans. Such countries are illustrated by Turkey and Jamaica. Although development institutions such as the World Bank and AID should maintain a presence in these countries, concessionary aid should be made available only when and if government policies become favorable for the effective employment of such assistance.

5. Countries which have high incomes and/or rapid growth based wholly on the export of a natural resource such as oil, which provides little direct development content.

Such countries usually require a great deal of advice and technical assistance which might well come from development institutions such as the World Bank on a loan basis. This group might be illustrated by Nigeria and Algeria. They should be expected to obtain the bulk of their external capital requirements from nonconcessionary sources.

In relating eligibility for aid to the adoption of policies conducive to growth, we recognize that in nearly all countries there will be a mixture of both favorable and unfavorable policies and that we are dealing with different shades of gray rather than black and white. Eligibility for concessionary aid is unlikely to be an all or nothing matter unless policies and perhaps internal political conditions are so bad that any aid is likely to be ineffective and perhaps counterproductive. The World Bank and IDA do not simply announce a cutoff of all assistance to a member in good standing, and for obvious reasons bilateral aid donors do not announce a termination of all assistance to friendly recipient countries. There is nearly always some assistance in the pipeline from earlier commitments and new requests for assistance are given consideration. The donor should take into account the policies of the recipients when appraising projects and the relationship of those projects to the effectiveness of aid. The denial of aid requests on the basis of such appraisals will, hopefully, have an impact on the country's policymakers.

Concessionary Aid for Countries that Need Only Capital

May there not be countries in our third and fourth categories identified above that do not require the technical and advisory components normally packaged with concessionary development assistance since they

already have the preconditions for growth and the
capacity for optimal allocation and use of capital for
promoting maximum growth? Should not such countries
receive aid in much the same way they would if they
were borrowing on the international financial markets,
provided they are otherwise eligible for concessionary
assistance?

In the first place, we are unlikely to find any
country, developing or developed, that could not use
objective advice or adopt more constructive policies.
Both bilateral and multilateral donor agencies provide
resources on a subsidized basis at the direct or indirect
expense of the public in the countries transferring
these resources, so that donor agencies have an obligation to see that the resources are employed in the
most efficient manner for the realization of the objectives. Moreover, if a government is following all the
right policies, is fully committed to development, and
possesses the institutions for maximum effective use of
capital, it is probably already enjoying a condition of
self-sustaining growth and can readily obtain additional
external capital for achieving a higher growth rate
from private international financial markets. It is
our view that simply supplying capital is not development
assistance, but making bank loans on subsidized terms.

The Case of Aborted Growth

Either progress toward, or the achievement of, the
condition of self-sustained growth itself may be aborted
for a variety of reasons. This could occur as a consequence of some external shock such as the sharp rise
in oil prices in 1974-75 and again in 1980, or other
long-term shifts in a country's terms of trade; or it
might occur as a consequence of unwise economic policies
leading to inflation and reduced export growth, or the
accumulation of large external debt incurred for public
expenditures without regard for the growth in exports
to service the debt. In the latter case growth could
be threatened by the necessity of reducing imports
essential for investment in order to maintain debt
service. Whether any of these contingencies leading to
aborted growth call for development assistance as contrasted with balance of payments assistance, such as
is provided by the IMF, is a question that will be
dealt with in the following chapter.

ESTABLISHING THE PRECONDITIONS
FOR SELF-SUSTAINED GROWTH

As we have already noted, developing countries
vary widely in the extent and nature of their preconditions for self-sustained growth. For example, the

bulk of the populations of many of the countries in the sub-Saharan region are just emerging from a primitive tribal status. In such cases development assistance must concentrate largely on institution building, training, and the design of projects that will over time reach a high proportion of those in rural agriculture. Although these projects require capital, including that for infrastructure such as roads and irrigation, there must be a large technical assistance component, even with relatively good policies and dedication on the part of the government. The success of these projects cannot always be measured by their short-run impact on the growth rate. This applies particularly to education and training programs and to social programs in the fields of health and sanitation that can be justified in terms of their impact on human productivity.

For the more advanced poor LDCs, such as those in the Indian subcontinent, development assistance also requires a substantial component dedicated to institution building and training, but the areas of major concern must be broadened to include not only agriculture, but the building of the industrial base with appropriate regard for both exporting and import substituting production. Governmental policies and the allocation of adequate government funds and competent personnel for the aid-supported programs are critical elements for success, but concessionary aid becomes more important in terms of supplementing domestic resources for private and governmental investment.

A third stage is represented by countries such as most of the Latin American countries that have achieved a substantial level of preconditions for sustained growth, but which require a period of development assistance to become self-sustaining. Although in this stage external capital as a supplement to domestic resources becomes the most important component of concessionary aid, the influence of the donor on overall resource allocation, the selection and design of specific projects, and on the policies of the recipient countries continues to be an essential part of development assistance.

In the fourth stage are countries that have acquired the capacity for sustained growth and a relatively high per capita income of, say, $1200 to $1500 in 1980 dollars. These countries should be expected to progress rapidly to a point at which all external capital is obtained on nonconcessionary terms, except possibly under conditions of aborted growth. Consequently, all concessionary aid should gradually fall to zero.

Korea is a good example of a country that had reached this fourth stage by the mid-1970s. In her study of the role of aid in the Korean development, Anne Krueger writes:

By the late 1960s commercial borrowing was replacing aid as the key form of foreign savings, while the domestic savings rate was rising rapidly. Whether commercial borrowing could have contributed anywhere near what it in fact did had aid earlier been in the form of loans other than grants is extremely doubtful. Whereas the aid of the 1950s constituted the bulk of available resources for capital formation, the foreign savings of the late 1960s and early 1970s were really a supplement to domestic savings, one that was critical to permit the high rate of growth Korea actually enjoyed in those years....In 1975 foreign savings financed investments equal to 10 percent of GNP, although most of that came from foreign loans.[2]

It would appear that given a per capita growth rate in the range of 10 percent and a per capita income of well over $1000, Korea had reached a condition of self-sustained growth by the second half of the 1970s.

THE POTENTIAL ROLE OF CONCESSIONARY AID
FOR ESTABLISHING PRECONDITIONS FOR GROWTH
IN SUB-SAHARAN AFRICA

Moderate success in agricultural performance and in raising growth rates in the Indian subcontinent, including Bangladesh, together with the widespread famine in sub-Saharan Africa in the 1970s have focused attention on the latter area as the major challenge for world development assistance agencies.[3] Despite a few successes in terms of per capita GNP growth, e.g., Kenya, Malawi and the Ivory Coast, 15 countries in this region had a negative rate of growth of per capita income during the 1960-1979 period, and in 19 countries per capita incomes grew by less than 1 percent per year. Without extraordinary measures, the outlook for the future is even worse. In the World Development Report 1981 the Low Case projection for an annual rate of growth in GDP for the sub-Sahara as a whole is 1.9 percent per year over the 1980-1990 period. Given a projected population growth of about 3 percent over the next two decades, this GDP growth rate projection translates into a negative per capita growth rate in excess of 1 percent per annum, and even the High Case projection for GDP growth rate of 3 percent would mean a zero per capita growth rate.[4]

A recent World Bank report entitled Accelerated Development in Sub-Saharan Africa: An Agenda for Action (1981) envisages the possibility of an annual rate of growth in GDP per capita in the 1980s in excess of 2 percent per year with a rise in agricultural output per capita of 3.8 percent per year, given the necessary policy reforms coupled with a prescribed level of foreign aid. Export performance would need to be reversed from a negative rate of growth in export volume during the 1970-1979 period to a positive rate of growth in excess of 5 percent for the 1980-1990 period. The requirements for growth, as contrasted with stagnation or decline with a continuation of present conditions, cover a range of measures with particular emphasis on agriculture, including both food production and export crops. They include increased productive efforts in private agriculture with the aid of inputs such as better seed, fertilizer, equipment, spare parts, agricultural credits, and irrigation (especially small irrigation projects created by the farmers themselves); better marketing facilities for cash crops, including feeder roads and transportation; technical assistance to farmers through extension services; and increased agricultural research for dealing with a number of problems peculiar to the crops and the regions. There must also be a rapid development of import-substituting, labor-intensive industry, of indigenous energy resources for the oil-importing countries, and of nonfuel mineral resources for expanding exports. Without further cataloging the physical production requirements, the World Bank report and other studies emphasize that governmental policy reform is the sine qua non for promoting indigenous private activity and assuring supplies of necessary inputs.

For most of these countries the educational and skill base for modern economic development is quite deficient. In countries whose populations number in the millions, there are often only a few thousand with a college education and less than 5 percent with a secondary education. Adult literacy is frequently under 15 percent and confined almost entirely to those in urban centers.

The World Bank report on sub-Saharan Africa states that "domestic issues are at the heart of the crisis, and no real turnaround is conceivable unless these policy matters are dealt with." Perhaps the most important policy changes relate to the trade and exchange rate system that are heavily biased against farmers, thereby reducing their incentive to produce food for both local consumption and export. The same trade and foreign exchange policies are biased against local industrial production and distort industrial development by encouraging import-intensive industry and discouraging the development of domestic industries that use local raw materials and labor. In addition to policy reforms, the administrative structure and capacity of the governments of the sub-Saharan countries must be substantially improved in order to carry out programs for supplying inputs, for improving markets, and for technical assistance required by the private agricultural sector and by industry.

It should be emphasized that no amount of concessionary aid can produce conditions for growth in the sub-Saharan region without institution building, technical training, and appropriate governmental policies and dedication. As is pointed out in the DAC 1981 Review (Chapter 3, paragraph 31), "The problem in the past has not so much been that the total volume of aid to the investment in low-income Africa have been low, compared with other regions; in Africa average productivity of investment and of aid has been lower than elsewhere. Donors contemplating feasible increments in their aid, therefore, will be strongly encouraged to make them only if and as certain accompanying conditions can be met--including in part by donors' own efforts." ODA to the oil-importing African countries rose from $1.6 billion (in 1978 dollars) to $4.3 billion in 1980, or at an average rate of about 10.5 percent. This compares with a rate of growth in ODA of about 5.5 percent (in 1978 dollars) over the 1970-1980 period for all oil-importing developing countries.

How Much Concessionary Aid is Needed for the Sub-Saharan Region?

Reports emanating from development assistance agencies tend to make growth projections on the basis of what is realistically possible for a country or region provided all the policy and institutional conditions are met, and then deduce the external assistance requirements for the most optimistic growth scenario. This is, of course, good strategy in seeking commitments from donors, but the fact is that the amounts of concessionary aid that can be effectively employed will not be known until a multi-year program for a particular country or region is being implemented. For example, the DAC 1981 Review (Chapter III) states that "Donors should strain to raise their contributions of aid provided there is some parallel African movement toward policy reform and provided the African donors jointly can mount a substantial augmentation of the Continent's capacity for developing expertise of the appropriate kind." The problem of estimating aid requirements is especially difficult in regions such as the sub-Sahara since establishing preconditions for growth should constitute the primary objective of development assistance and neither the outcomes of a series of multi-phased programs or the time periods required can be known in advance. The cost of programs under ideal conditions can be estimated, but only time will tell how much aid can be effectively used.

Without attempting to judge the amounts of aid that can be usefully employed, it is clear that concessionary aid is needed for carrying out programs for stimulating private agriculutral and industrial sector development in accordance with the general recommend- ations of the World Bank report on the sub-Saharan region. Increased incentives for expanding the produc- tion of cash crops (and in some cases transferring labor out of subsistence production) may prove ineffec- tive unless farmers can acquire the basic inputs and unless there exist facilities for transporting and marketing the output. The shopping list of commodities and services outlined in the previous paragraphs includes a high proportion of imports. Because of the close dependence of external resources on administrative im- provements for stimulating growth, external aid requires a large input of technical assistance by the donors. There is also need for better coordination among the bilateral and multilateral donors operating in the re- gion, a requirement emphasized in the DAC 1981 Review.

Since most of the countries of the sub-Saharan region lack the debt service capacity and credit standing to increase substantially their nonconcessionary bor- rowing,[5] aid must mainly take the form of ODA. More- over, the rise in oil prices in 1980-81 and the fall in world prices of many important raw material exports of the region are likely to work against a favorable balance of payments outlook for these countries.

Although a discussion of the methodology of aid administration is beyond the terms of reference of the present report, we believe that foreign aid for the sub- Saharan region can be successful in promoting growth only if it is oriented to stimulating the private sector. This cannot be achieved in the absence of a willingness on the part of African governments to change their policy orientation which is all too frequently based on an ideology favoring state ownership and control. The political difficulties of changing this orientation are obvious.[6]

For many Arican countries the fundamental social and institutional conditions for broadly based develop- ment and, therefore, for self-sustaining growth cannot be acquired for many decades regardless of foreign exchange availablility. This is amply demonstrated by some of the oil-exporting countries where a modern urban sector has been super-imposed on an essentially primitive society on which many years of almost unlimited foreign exchange resources have made little real impact. Since for many African countries the economic and social basis for sustained growth at even a relatively low level of living by Western standards will require many decades, the principal emphasis of development assistance should be on education, training, technical assistance and institution building. In this context establishing growth targets as goals for concessionary aid programs may be misplaced. A more relevant material

goal for the near future might be to enable these
countries to provide for themselves sufficient food,
sanitation and shelter for minimum comfort and avoidance
of human suffering. The large capital-intensive, urban
oriented projects should probably be delayed, at least
as candidates for ODA.

NOTES

1 World Development Report 1981, op.cit., Table
1, pp. 134-135.

2 Development Role of the Foreign Sector,
op.cit., p. 212.

3 This focus on sub-Saharan Afica is illustrated
by Chapter 2, entitled "Focus on Africa," in the DAC
1980 Review, followed by special attention given to
that region in the DAC 1981 Review. The development
problems of sub-Saharan Africa are also the subject of
a comprehensive World Bank document entitled Accelerated Development in Sub-Saharan Africa: An Agenda
for Action, Washington, DC: World Bank, 1981.

4 World Development Report 1981, op.cit., p. 15.
A per capita growth rate of zero for the Low Case and
0.3 percent for the High Case is given for the 1980-1990
period on p. 3 of the Report, but this does not appear
to be consistent with the projections of GDP growth for
the region given on p. 15, assuming the World Bank projection of 3 percent population growth. However, it is
possible that a negative per capita income growth rate
would reduce the population growth rate as a consequence
of malnutrition and increased child death rates.

5 In 1980 the overall debt-service ratio of the
lowincome oil-importing countries of the region was 19.2
percent (up from 10.4 percent in 1978), and six countries had recourse to multilateral debt renegotiations
in 1978-1980.

6 This problem is recognized and discussed can-
didly in the 1981 Review, DAC, op.cit., paragraph 32.

5
Assessing the Effectiveness
of Concessionary Aid
for Promoting Economic Growth

In this chapter we are concerned specifically with assessing the effectiveness of concessionary aid in promoting the condition of self-sustained growth. Since progress toward this condition involves many factors, most of which are outside the direct control of the aid donors, the attribution problem in analyzing the contribution of concessionary aid to both successes and failures becomes exceedingly difficult. In most cases concessionary aid is a marginal input in the process. Economists have learned a great deal from comparative studies of development about the preconditions for development; about the factors contributing to incentives and other conditions for stimulating output and productivity in various sectors; about the allocation of investment for achieving a viable pattern of growth for external equilibrium; and about governmental policies that encourage or discourage savings, production, and the allocation of investment in proper channels. We also know that specified aid-supported projects can support and supplement domestic resources for making investments that might not otherwise be made; influence the choice and design of investment projects; provide research, program guidance and technical assistance for institution building; provide training or initiate training programs at various levels; and influence general governmental policies. We can often make estimates, however crude, of the micro-contributions of specific aid-supported projects or programs, but we are far less able to assess the macro-contributions of aid to growth.

Several studies have examined the relationship between foreign aid or capital imports and the economic performance of developing countries.[1] Crosswell reviews these studies and concludes that the "evidence... on the importance of foreign assistance in achieving accelerated growth is ambiguous, in part because the experience of various countries and regions was mixed, and in part because there is not a clearly valid methodology for identifying the contribution of increased foreign assistance to accelerated growth, or the lack of foreign assistance to slow growth."[2]

The weaknesses of cross-section studies of the relationship between foreign aid and economic growth are all too apparent. If we are going to be able to say anything with confidence about this relationship, we must study the performance of individual countries and show specifically how particular aid programs have influenced the performance of particular sectors, improved the capacities of the economic agents through education and training, removed bottlenecks, or influenced government policies.

The problem of assessing the general effectiveness of ODA was addressed by DAC Chairman John P. Lewis in the 1980 Review, DAC.[3] In his thoughtful essay, Lewis raises a number of conceptual and analytical issues, including the problem of attributing the contribution of a marginal input to the complex process of development. After examining in a somewhat philosophical way the issues relating to aid effectiveness, Lewis reaches the conclusion that "None of the foregoing can, at this particular juncture, reflect the fact that ODA volume is the bottom-line issue."[4] But in the absence of better evidence than Lewis is able to provide on overall aid effectiveness, we do not see how he can answer categorically the question of whether current ODA volume is too much or too little.

The DAC 1981 Review contains a further discussion of aid effectiveness. Lewis concludes that "If one is prepared to settle for practical probabilities...the effectiveness case for present and prospective development assistance can be very powerful." However, he also reports that at the 1980 High Level meeting of the DAC "participants quite rightly underlined the continuing need to marshall unvarnished assessments of the consequences of past aid that can be fed back into the policy debate." In support of this objective, the DAC 1981 Review describes the work of a committee established "to test the hypothesis advanced in the DAC's 1980 meetings...namely, that the internal evaluation findings of members of aid agencies may now have reached a scale, level of professionalism and degree of potential comparability that permit one, by aggregating large amounts of this work, to say something about the cumulative impacts of substantial portions of aid over quite broad areas."[5] By bringing together the evaluations of projects and programs in particular sectors and in individual countries that have been assisted by a number of bilateral donors and multilateral agencies, the DAC group plans to evaluate the combined impact of aid from various sources on these sectors. These evaluations should enable the group to reach some quantitative estimates of the effectiveness of aid on the overall development progress of individual countries.

This large undertaking involving several members of the OECD Secretariat plus World Bank personnel contemplates a review of the evaluations of hundreds of projects and programs assisted by foreign aid over a period of several years. The results of this comprehensive program will, hopefully, provide a better basis for answering such questions as how effective is foreign aid in promoting economic growth and just how and under what conditions has it been effective? Obviously the resources available for the present study cannot begin to duplicate a large effort of this kind. Our effort will be limited to outlining methodologies for determining whether particular categories of concessionary aid programs have a high probability of making a positive contribution to economic growth.

AN APPROACH TO APPRAISING THE EFFECTIVENESS OF CONCESSIONARY AID IN PROMOTING ECONOMIC GROWTH

Our approach to appraising the effectiveness of concessionary aid for promoting growth will be oriented to particular types of aid-supported projects and programs. The assessment of overall effectiveness of perhaps hundreds of aid-supported activities in individual countries over a sufficient period of time to produce measurable progress toward self-sustained growth must await the collection, aggregation and analysis of ex post audits of aid-supported activities in dozens of countries. In considerable measure our approach parallels that of the World Bank's Performance Audit Reports from which much of the empirical evidence summarized in the following chapter is drawn.

One difficulty with a disaggregated approach is that if an aid-supported program or project is to contribute to growth, it will do so in interaction with other growth-generating activities. This must be considered in evaluating its effectiveness. In addition, the long-run effectiveness of any aid-supported program must be considered in terms of its capacity to generate the financing the institutional-building potential for expanding the supported activity itself, both over time and into other areas of the economy. In other words, the capacity for self-generation should be built into the aid-supported activities themselves. For example, if an aid-supported program succeeds in increasing the productivity of 10,000 farmers but no provision is made for continuing the program and for expanding it to several hundred thousand or a million farmers, it will lack the self-generating characteristic, and its contribution to self-sustained growth may be minimal.

Economic Returns from a Project

A basic criterion of aid effectiveness is the internal rate of return on the aid-supported project and every effort should be made to measure the economic return even for projects that yield no direct financial income. In most cases the aid component is only a fraction of the total value of the project so that the internal rate of return largely measures the return on domestic capital resources. The criterion for judging the appropriateness of the internal rate of return should be the social opportunity cost of domestic capital. If the internal rate of return is substantially less than the social opportunity cost of capital, there is obviously a misallocation of domestic resources, unless there are important positive externalities not included in the calculation of the internal rate of return. It might be argued that it is better to have domestic capital invested in a low-yielding project than not have any investment take place. However, this is not the realistic alternative. The very concept of the social opportunity cost of capital implies that there are alternative uses of the capital which will yield a certain return, and we should not simply assume that these resources will not be invested. The opportunity cost of capital for a country will always be at least equal to what capital could earn by investing it abroad. Moreover, if investments were made that yield returns well below the social opportunity cost of capital, it is unlikely that sufficient revenues from the project would be reinvested to maintain it or expand it in line with demand, and therefore its contribution to self-sustained growth would be impaired. The World Bank project audit of performance results employ a real internal rate of return of 10 percent as the criterion for determining the economic success or failure of a project, but most of the World Bank-supported projects have yielded much higher returns, and the loan appraisals for projects supported by the World Bank usually indicate internal rates in excess of 15 percent.

There are, of course, many aid-supported projects and programs for which estimates of economic returns, either for purposes of appraising projects or for ex post evaluation, are exceedingly difficult, but techniques have been developed for estimating the social rate of return on most any type of project. In some cases it may be necessary to estimate the social returns from a number of inter-related projects together since it may be impossible to determine the contribution of individual components. In any case, an inadequate estimate or range is better than no estimate at all. If it is believed there is no way whatsoever of estimating the returns from a proposed project or group of related

projects, there is a real question whether there exists
a sufficient argument to support it!

Financial Returns

Calculation of internal rates of return on projects
or programs often requires estimates of social returns
as is the case for example with education. However, in
the case of electric power, telecommunications and rail-
roads, for which the payments of services are made by
users, an important criterion is that revenues be high
enough not only to provide for operating and replacement
costs of the facilities, but for their expansion in line
with the expected growth of demand. This criterion is
in line with the concept of self-sustaining growth in
the sectors that are supported by aid and with the principle that domestic saving should over time replace foreign capital inflow.

Increased Productivity of Human, Material and Financial Resources

The contributions of aid-supported projects to increased productivity must be measured in a variety of
ways that may not be additive. For agricultural projects
the contribution may be measured by increased output,
a better mix of products for achieving higher value output, an increase in output per farmer or per acre of
land, and increased employment. In industry the contribution is reflected in increased output and employment,
higher productivity, and a better mix of output as between import substitution and production for the export
market. The contribution of infrastracture projects
such as power and transportation must be judged in terms
of their complementary inputs to the directly productive
activities of industry, mineral extraction, and agriculture, including reductions in cost. Power, water,
sewage projects, and highways also provide direct benefits to consumers, but if projects eligible for aid
support are to be given priority in terms of their contribution to growth, their effect on production rather
than on consumption must be given greater weight. Consumption per se should not be subsidized by aid, say, in
the form of assistance to power projects which services
go mainly to households, or to freeways used mainly by
domestic tourists. On the other hand, some social projects can be justified in terms of their effects on productivity; this may be the case with projects for
supplying clean water and health facilities. Aid-
supported rural development projects should be judged
particularly on the basis of their expected contribution
to output and not on the basis of their effects on dis-
tributional equity. However, we believe that by and

large output maximization will prove to be compatible
with the objective of alleviating absolute poverty.

Institution Building

Self-sustaining growth requires private and governmental institutions that will not only assure the success of individual projects no matter how financed, but
will be able to undertake the preparation, appraisal
and implementation of a series of projects designed to
enhance output and productivity. Institution building,
including staff training, should be a vital part of any
foreign aid program which contributes to self-sustained
growth. It is particularly important in the agriculutral
sector where programs of agriculutral credit, technical
assistance, seed and fertlilizer distribution and irrigation require institutional arrangements for the staff-
ing and training of extension services for reaching thousands of farmers and eventually many millions of farmers
as the programs are multiplied and expanded throughout
the country. A recent World Bank review of project performance audits estimated that 32 of the World Bank's
agricultural projects in nearly as many countries
(mostly initiated in the 1970s) and costing about $1.7
billion had reached 1.8 million farm families. However,
there is need for agricultural development programs to
reach several hundred million farmers in the low-income
countries, organized and financed largely without foreign aid by indigenous private and governmental organizations. The programs initiated by concessionary aid
should provide the institutional foundations and the
models for the longer-term effort required to stimulate
agricultural productivity and output throughout an entire country. To the maximum extent feasible the institutional arrangements should involve private firms and
cooperative organizations participated in by the farmer
beneficiaries.

Institution building is also of critical significance for loans to development finance corporations
(DFCs) for making subloans to small- and medium-sized
firms. Not only should DFCs have the capacity to channel funds to projects that will have a maximum impact
on growth, but these institutions should over time be
able to attract domestic capital for expanding their
operations to many times the level of the initial foreign aid.

Infrastructure projects such as those for power
and transportation also require an institutional and
technical assistance component when supported by aid.
For example, the managerial, accounting and maintenance
capacities may spell the difference between successful
and unsuccessful aid programs to these projects. Again
the institutional building component should be regarded
as part of the self-sustaining nature of the output. As

demand grows additional capacity should be financed out of past revenues and from the domestic capital market rather than with new concessionary loans.

Policy Reform

Appropriate policy changes should <u>precede</u> the implementation of a foreign aid program. Donors should not rely on promises that the policy changes essential for the success of aid-supported projects will be made at some politically convenient time in the future. Experience, as revealed by the audits of aid-supported projects we have reviewed, has shown that the promises are frequently not kept. Adopting the correct policies is an indication of a government's commitment to a project or program supported by foreign assistance. Policy reform is a measure of aid effectiveness since it not only affects the outcome of aid-supported projects, but of other activities essential for self-sustained growth.

The Problem of Aid Coordination

The approach to aid effectiveness outlined above implicitly assumes that aid to individual countries comes from a single donor who is in the position to allocate foreign aid on the basis of the criteria which have been set forth. Actually there are often many donors operating in a single country, including possibly several bilateral donors plus the World Bank Group, and a regional development bank such as the IADB or ADB. There may be several donors involved in the same sector in an individual country. This condition may reduce the effectiveness of aid and the influence on policies and institutional building by any single donor. The need for greater policy coordination is a major theme of the annual DAC reports and other treatises on the foreign aid establishment. This is a complex issue beyond the terms of reference of this report, but not the least of the problems arises from the fact that different donors have different objectives.

THE EFFECTIVENESS OF CONCESSIONARY AID FOR STRUCTURAL ADJUSTMENT

A substantial amount of financial assistance from the IMF, the World Bank and IDA has been provided for "structural adjustment assistance." In fiscal 1980 the World Bank and IDA inaugurated a program of "lending designed to support major changes in policy and institutions of developing countries that would reduce their current account deficits to more manageable proportions in the medium term while maintaining the maximum feasible development effort."[6] Such lending "consists of financial support for specified programs of monitorable and time-bound policy action by governments. It is therefore unlike project lending in which the needs of the project tend to dominate the timing and preparation and appraisal of an operation and in which disbursement of Bank funds is linked to project implementation."

Since the beginning of this program to the end of calendar 1981 the World Bank made $1.4 billion in structural adjustment loans to about a dozen countries, including Korea ($250 million), Bolivia ($50 million), Kenya ($55 million), Malawi ($45 million), the Philippines ($200 million), and Turkey (two loans totalling $500 million). According to a press statement by the World Bank,[7] to qualify for structural adjustment lending:

> A country must be willing to adopt changes in its policies, programs and institutions that will help its economy adapt to the harsher economic environment of the 1980s--adverse terms of trade, recession rates, and creditworthiness problems. This means reducing the current account deficit to a level commensurate with the amount of external concessionary and commercial capital to which the country can expect to have access, without straining its debt service capacity. A series of loans is therefore called for in order to monitor the implementation of previously agreed actions and in order to provide support for subsequent stages of the reform. Since circumstances vary from country to country, no two programs of structural adjustment are alike, but there is a general need to improve agricultural and industrial efficiency, to promote the expansion and diversification of exports, and of import saving activities on the basis of comparative advantage, to develop domestic energy resources more vigorously and improve the efficiency of their use, and to raise domestic savings rates. The foreign exchange made available through structural adjustment lending is used to pay for general imports, excluding such items as arms and luxury goods.

The funds are quickly disbursed, and the repayment terms are the same as those for the regular project operations -- 15 to 20 years for the World Bank and 50 years for IDA.

Beginning in 1974 the IMF inaugurated a program of enlarged access to its resources in excess of the credit tranches in cases where the member "requires a relatively long period of adjustment and a maximum period for repurchase longer than the three to five years specified under normal standby arrangement."[8] Such assistance differs from the traditional concept of IMF balance of payments assistance designed to deal with deficits arising from temporary but reversible external factors, or deficits originating from internal monetary and fiscal policies that are amenable to fiscal and monetary restraint and exchange rate adjustment.

Structural adjustment assistance was introduced mainly in response to the so-called "external shocks" that occurred during the 1970s. These are largely attributed to the sharp increase in oil prices, but some countries such as the metal exporters experienced a substantial deterioration in their terms of trade as a consequence of the sharp fall in prices of base metals. There have also been reductions in export volume as a consequence of the world recession, but deficits arising from cyclical movements are normally dealt with by drawing down official reserves and intermediate-term borrowing from the IMF. The World Development Report 1981 gives the following estimates of terms of trade effects as a percentage of GNP (1974-1978 average) for the following country groupings: all LDC oil importers, 0.90; primary producing LDCs, 1.65; populous South Asia, 1.26; and least developed, 0.14. It is clear from these figures that the adverse terms of trade effects on GNP were almost negligible for the least developed countries for the 1974-1978 period. In the case of primary producing countries, much of the terms of trade effect arose from the decline in their export prices.[9]

Ways of Adjusting to External Shocks

The World Development Report identifies three basic ways in which countries have responded to external shocks during the 1970s: (a) structural adjustment, which includes switching resources to the production of exports and import substitutes, including domestic substitutes for imported energy; (b) external financing; and (c) slower growth, which narrows current account deficits by restricting imports. Of those countries relying heavily on structural adjustment, the most successful were the countries following an outward-oriented approach leading to an expansion of exports (e.g., South Korea). Those countries following an inward-oriented approach relied more heavily on external borrowing (e.g., Turkey). By and large the countries with an outward orientation, including both semi-industrial countries and primary producing countries, maintained their growth rates, while those following inward orientation had reduced growth rates. The outward-oriented economies used external financing to cover increases in prices of imports until they were able to pay for them with increased exports. In these countries "most of the extra investment needed to effect adjustment was financed by increased domestic saving, and their strong export performance meant that debt service ratios rose only slightly. By contrast, reliance on external borrowing was significantly greater in the inward-looking group which did not undertake structural adjustment."10

India's growth rate rose from 3.4 percent in 1964-1973 to 4.3 percent in 1974-1979 despite the sharp rise in oil prices. Adjustment was promoted by the achievement of near self-sufficiency in food grains and a rise in migrants' remittances. There was also a higher level of aid.11

In the case of the least developed countries (LLDCs), deterioration in the terms of trade was relatively unimportant, although they did experience a slow growth in the market for their primary products. Much more important than the "external shock was the decline in their export market shares which was caused by domestic failures, particularly in agriculture."12

Although the above analysis taken from the World Development Report does not include the 80 percent real increase in petroleum prices in 1979-80, certain conclusions stand out from the 1974-1978 experience. First, adjustment to the rise in oil prices and other external shocks during the 1970s was not the major problem for the LLDCs, such as those in sub-Saharan Africa. Second, countries that followed outward-oriented policies, while initially benefitting from external capital flows, were able to adjust readily without reducing their growth rates and without increasing foreign borrowing at a rate faster than the growth in their exports. In other words, their international credit standing was not impaired by a rapidly rising debt service-export earnings ratio.

It should be pointed out that the term "structural adjustment assistance" is often misused or employed ambiguously. If structural adjustment assistance has a special meaning that distinguishes it from the general concept of development assistance on the one hand and normal IMF balance of payments assistance on the other, it must relate to a sudden change in world markets or to some exogenous internal development such as war, civil disturbance or natural disaster which requires special development strategies and policies for adjustment to the new conditions. Under such conditions increased external resources can ease the adjustment process by maintaining imports while the required adjustment measures are taking effect; but the term structural adjustment has been employed to include a condition of balance of payments equilibrium caused by excessive public expenditures financed by fiscal deficits (as was the case with the justification of structural assistance to the Ivory Coast), or even a condition of low growth in general. For example, the statement in the World Development Report 1981 that "low-income countries require long-term external finance for adjustment" constitutes a use of the term adjustment to mean the creation of conditions for sustained growth (which they have never attained) and not adjustment to external shocks which was the theme of the material discussed in the earlier portion of the same chapter entitled "Country Experience: Managing Adjustment."[13]

THE DEVELOPMENT COMPONENT OF STRUCTURAL ADJUSTMENT

Since both the IMF and the World Bank (and IDA) have been providing assistance for structural adjustment, questions have been raised regarding the appropriate roles of the IMF and the development institutions. Public statements by officials of the two institutions have dealt with this question by stating that the Bank is recognized as having primary responsibility for "the composition and appropriateness of development programs and project evaluations, including development priorities," while the Fund is "recognized as having primary responsibility for exchange rates and restrictive systems, for adjustment of temporary balance of payment disequilibrium, and for evaluating and assisting members to work out stabilization programs as a sound basis for economic advance." As is sometimes stated by these sources, the Fund is primarily concerned with "macroeconomic variables relating to monetary, fiscal, foreign borrowing and exchange policies," while the Bank has responsibility for "microeconomic factors" such as the composition of development programs, project evaluation and development priorities. Since both institutions are currently concerned with achieving the same objective, namely, balance of payments adjustment of a structural or longer-term nature, and since the correction of a balance of payment disequilibrium requires both macro- and microeconomic analysis and recommendations for adjustment, the staffs of the two institutions have agreed on methods and areas of collaboration where one or both agencies are involved in assisting a member.

Before commenting on the contribution of concessionary aid for structural adjustment to self-sustained growth, we shall examine briefly the development component in structural adjustment, the support of which is the appropriate function of development assistance. Let us assume that a country with an initial current account balance experiences a sharp reduction in its terms of trade, as would be the case with a substantial rise in imported oil prices. There is an immediate rise in absorption (A), or what the country consumes (C) and invests (I), relative to national output (Y), and the current account (B) becomes negative.

Thus, Y < A so that Y - A = -B   or Y - (C+I) = -B.

One way to restore balance is to reduce A by
reducing C or I, but this is likely to reduce Y since
consumers and investors curtail their demand for output.
However, if the structure of both absorption and output
can be shifted, it is possible to reduce A without
reducing Y. What is required is for output to shift
from nontradeable goods to tradeable goods so that the
decline in demand for nontradeable goods as a consequence
of the reduction in A will be offset by an increase in
the demand for tradeables from both foreign buyers and
from domestic buyers of import substitutes. This process is called "switching" and it involves a shift in
both the pattern of domestic production and the pattern
of internal demand as between imports and import substitution. It also involves an increase in exports
relative to imports.

Demand switching in the face of a reduction in A
can be achieved through changes in relative prices as
between imports and domestic substitutes and between
domestic prices and foreign prices. These changes in
relative prices can be brought about by exchange rate
adjustments. However, output switching may require
more time and some increase in investment. But if
investment must rise while absorption declines, consumption may have to be reduced beyond the limits of public
tolerance. Therefore, it is argued that the additional
investment required for output switching must be supplied from external sources. It is sometimes further
argued that in the case of very poor countries where
consumption by a large proportion of the population is
already at the basic subsistence level, external capital
should maintain consumption as well as provide the additional capital requirements for adjusting the pattern
of output.

The process of switching described above can generally be handled rather easily if there exists a relatively high rate of growth and a high level of investment.
Investment can be shifted from non-tradeable industries
to those producing for export or import substitution,
and the impact on consumption can be limited to some
reduction in its rate of growth, with any immediate
decline avoided by capital imports. But where growth
and investment are stagnating, an absolute reduction
in consumption may be required unless supported by
foreign aid.

It should be made clear in this analysis that in
order to achieve internal and external balance simul-
taneously, both a reduction in absorption and switching
are required. In a recent World Bank staff paper F.Z.
Jaspersen stated "Absorption reduction without switching will result in a decline in output and increased
unemployment. Switching without absorption reduction

will achieve neither internal nor external balance. If domestic demand in not reduced, excess demand will be created for nontradeable goods, prices will rise in that sector and the policy-induced change in relative prices will be eliminated."[14] However, in the case of a country experiencing a high rate of growth, both absorption reduction and switching can be achieved within a relatively short period of time with little more than a temporary dampening of the rate of growth of consumption. This is well illustrated by the experience of Korea in dealing with the rise in oil prices during the 1973-1976 period.[15]

The above analysis suggests that the proper role of development assistance agencies in structural adjustment lies in supporting investments in industry and agriculture that produce tradeables, including sources of energy that substitute for imported oil. It might be stated that for most developing countries the requirements for structural adjustment differ little from those required for self-sustained growth even in the absence of external shocks. This is true because of the importance of exports in generating growth and of the fact that most developing countries need to improve their current account positions. The appropriate policies for reducing absorption and of inducing both demand and supply switching must be followed or internal and external balance will not be achieved. These policies include exchange rate depreciation, monetary and fiscal restraint, and the elimination of price controls where they exist. The repercussions of these policies on the economy may be softened by IMF credits provided under a standby agreement that specifies the appropriate policies.

The Effectiveness of Structural Adjustment Loans for Development

Although the respective roles of the World Bank Group and the IMF in the structural adjustment process can be delineated conceptually, in practice the contribution of World Bank program loans the proceeds of which are not tied to projects or sectors cannot be distinguished from that of IMF credits. Where there is close collaboration between the Bank and the IMF with both providing financial assistance to a country for achieving structural balance, will not the principal function of the Bank's structural loan be that of supplementing the IMF standby credit? Although it is true that the World Bank negotiates an agreement with the recipient country covering general development policies, priorities and objectives, the Bank will lack the policy instruments it exercises in the case of project or multi-project or even sector loans. Moreover, when the Bank makes a project or sector program loan

covering a number of individual projects, it has lever-
age over the allocation of resources several times the
amount of its own financial commitment, but program
loans for structural adjustment simply finance imports
for any and all economic purposes. We must ask therefore: Where is the institution building, the technical
assistance and training, the project or program formulation or appraisal, and other specific contributions
to sustained growth that should constitute the essence
of development assistance? All that exists is a promise
on the part of the recipient country to follow what the
Bank conceives as sound development policy in restoring
internal and external balance.

We are not suggesting that the $250 million struc-
tural adjustment loan made to Korea in December 1981
will not be accompanied by sound financial and development policies that will support the restoration of
equilibrium.[16] However, we suspect that the Bank's
development input into Korea's structural adjustment
will be little different than if Korea had borowed
funds in the Eurocurrency market. At the same time the
World Bank made a loan of $90 million to Korea to expand
its urban water supply, but presumably, in the implementation of this loan, the Bank exercises direct development
assistance functions.

We have no doubt that for some countries such as
Korea structural adjustment loans can be shown to have
a long-term impact on the rate of growth since the
loans may make it unnecessary for the recipients to
reduce the level of their investments or even the rate
of growth of their investments in the course of the
balance of payments adjustment process. Such countries
have the capacity for self-sustained growth and can be
counted on to make the adjustments required for continued
development progress. What they require is not development assistance, but balance of payments support.
Can we say the same for Turkey, Guyana, Senegal, Bolivia
and other countries at a lower level of development that
have received structural adjustment loans? May not the
availability of structural adjustment loans enable them
to delay internal adjustment measures? Structural adjustment loans from development agencies may also weaken
the influence of the IMF on countries' macroeconomic
policies. In both of these cases the structural adjustment loans could prove to be counterproductive.

Finally, it should be said that our concerns
regarding the effectiveness of structural adjustment
loans reflect the rather poor results of program loans
and general industrial import credits which the World
Bank and IDA have made in the past in terms of the
willingness of the recipients to undertake policy reforms
contained in the loan agreements. These results are
discussed in the following chapter.

NOTES

1 See, for example, Hollis Chenery and N. Carter, "Foreign Assistance and Development Performance, 1960-1970," American Economic Review, May 1973; G.F. Papanek, "The Effect of Aid and Other Resource Transfers on Savings and Growth in Less Developed Countries," Economic Journal, September 1979; and Theodore Lewis and Constantine Michalopoulos, "Developing Country's Growth: Projections, Performance and Implications for a New International Development Strategy," AID (mimeo), Washington, DC: US Department of State, January 1980.

2 Crosswell, "Growth, Poverty Alleviation," op.cit., p. 207.

3 1980 Review, DAC, op.cit., pp. 53-69.

4 Ibid., p. 65.

5 1981 Review, DAC, op.cit., Chapter 2.

6 World Bank Annual Report 1980, Washington, DC: World Bank, pp. 69-70.

7 IMF Survey, Washington, DC: IMF, December 14, 1981, pp. 395-396.

8 Annual Report 1981, Washington, DC: International Monetary Fund, p. 86.

9 World Development Report 1981, p. 66.

10 World Development Report 1981, op.cit., p. 75.

11 Ibid., pp. 79-80.

12 Ibid., pp. 81-82.

13 World Development Report 1981, op.cit., Chapter 6, p. 82.

14 Adjustment Experience and Growth Prospects of the Semi-Industrial Economies, World Bank Staff Working Paper No. 477, Washington, DC, August 1981, pp. 13-14.

15 Ibid., p. 50.

16 "World Bank Clears South Korea Loans of $340 Million," Wall Street Journal, December 22, 1981, p. 29.

6
Tentative Observations on the Results of Aid-Supported Projects and Programs Based on Performance Audits

The following commentaries on aid-supported projects and programs are based on a limited number of case histories and of appraisals of aid-supported projects and programs by officials of aid institutions, including the World Bank and AID, and by private research groups and individuals. Since most of the official appraisals made available to the authors are confidential, we cannot reveal the name of the aid recipient or the sources of the information. However, we have referenced a few appraisals published by AID. Owing to the limited sample, our observations must necessarily be tentative and are in no sense firm conclusions that can be adequately supported by the evidence. Although we find that certain forms of aid or aid-supported projects are frequently subject to criticism in terms of the potential realization of one or more of their objectives, we do not deny that there are examples of successful aid programs based on each of the modalities that we review. Nevertheless, our limited empirical findings support some of our major a priori conclusions.

THE AGRICULTURAL SECTOR

Most of the success stories of concessionary aid have occurred in agricultural programs. For example, one of the largest recipients of agricultural aid from the World Bank, IDA and AID has been India. In the early 1970s India was importing over 10 million tons of grain each year, but by the second half of the 1970s India had become largely self-sufficient in food grains. Undoubtedly concessionary aid played a large role in this outcome, but there have been dozens of external programs sponsored by different agencies covering many essential components of agricultural activity. There was the "Green Revolution" technology which combined the controlled use of water with improved seed, fertilizers, and appropriate mechanization, and there were the extension and other programs that brought this technology and the necessary inputs to hundreds of thousands of farms. There were the programs to improve marketing, including the building of roads linking villages and market towns, and the agricultural credit programs for small farmers. There were also a number of irrigation programs, many of them undertaken by the farmers themselves with external assistance; the area irrigated by modern pump wells in India increased almost ten-fold between 1964 and 1975. The Indian government played a major role both in the implementation of the programs and improved policies relating to product prices and the deregulation of the distribution of ferti- lizers.

It is difficult, of course, to disaggregate the contribution of the various external and internal assist- ance programs to the development of India's agriculture and so far as we are aware no one has attempted this task.

There have been a wide variety of aid-supported agricultural and rural development programs. Some have taken the form of loans to governments for financing imported inputs such as fertilizers, seeds, livestock, tractors and other farm equipment, and irrigation equip- ment with little direct involvement by the donor agency in the agricultural sector. Other programs have involved the transfer of agricultural inputs, credit, and tech- nical assistance to the individual farmers with sub- stantial involvement by the aid agency. The success of the various programs in terms of expanding agricul- tural output has depended heavily on the price incentives and marketing opportunities provided the farmers; the institutional arrangements and competence of domestic personnel for transferring the material inputs and technical knowledge to the farmers; and the technical design of the program for determining the right inputs for increasing productivity and output mix. Program design is also important for obtaining the maximum participation of farmers in the target area.

Aid programs that do little more than provide governments with foreign exchange to enable the agri- cultural sector to acquire imported inputs through the usual distribution channels have frequently not proved successful, especially in countries lacking precon- ditions for growth. They serve mainly to influence recipient countries employing foreign exchange controls to allocate more foreign exchange to satisfy the import demands of the agricultural sector. In many cases governments have been required by the donor agency to establish local currency counterpart funds to carry out investment programs in the agricultural sector, but these investment programs are frequently not speci- fied and in general have not been successful in expand- ing farm output. The greater availability of farm inputs may or may not result in inputs going to farmers that will make the most productive use of them at prices they can afford or are willing to pay.

Market Access

The success of any program for raising agricultural output depends upon product price incentives, marketing organization, and the availability of transportaiton at reasonable cost to the markets. Transportation is especially important for small farms that are located in isolated mountainous areas. In 1975 AID approved a loan to Colombia for the construction by labor-intensive methods of roads in a mountainous section of Colombia. The project is called Pico Y Pala (pick and shovel) and by 1980 more than 50 roads had been built linking isolated homes and villages with markets in nearby towns. Since transport costs sometimes represented as much as 80 percent of the market value of the products, the farmers switched from subsistence farming to production of commodities for the market and greatly expanded their output from both more intensive and more extensive cultivation. The roads also provided the opportunity for access to fertilizer and improved seed and access to credit where available. Unfortunately the Colombian government agencies responsible for various types of agricultural technical assistance did not expand their activities into the areas served by the new roads.

Although the AID Project Evaluation Report found the project highly effective in expanding agriculutral output and incomes of small farmers, even in the absence of increased technical assistance, it reported that the government failed to provide the funding for expanding the program in accordance with the original plan and, in addition, arrangements had not been made for funding the maintenance of the roads.[1] At the time of the evaluation the project, however valuable its initial impact, did not provide the conditions for self-generating replication.

In 1964 AID made grants totalling $65 million to assist rural road construction in Thailand with concentration on the more isolated areas of the country. The impact of the roads on agriculutrual production was found to be substantial in terms of both the volume of output and the mix of farm products. An AID Project Evaluation Report also stressed the institution building contribution to the Thailand Accelerated Rural Development Program which is continuing to provide basic infrastructure and economic and social services for the rural areas.[2]

Irrigation Programs

Irrigation programs have made a substantial contribution to agricultural output in developing countries
in recent decades, and Montague Yudelman estimates
that 40 percent of all increases in rice yields in
Asia over the 1965-1975 period can be attributed to an
expansion of irrigation. He points out that irrigation
is the largest single component of World Bank lending
in agriculture and refers to a number of projects
where such support has been successful.[3] Our review
of the appraisal reports on loans for irrigation projects reveals that the most successful have been the
decentralized programs that provide equipment for farmers to dig their own wells with the advantage of
technical assistance from extension services rather
than the large centralized projects, a number of which
have been poorly designed and poorly managed.

In 1975 AID initiated financial and technical
assistance support of Philippine government programs
to expand village irrigation systems. Local irrigation
associations were formed with the support of the National
Farm System Development Corporation, the AID-funded
implementing agency. Rice yields increased in part as
a consequence of the opportunity for double cropping.
Although gross farm income doubled and in some cases
tripled with the installation of irrigation systems and
improved water distribution, costs increased even more
rapidly as a consequence of the cost of elecricity,
fuel, fertilizer, credits, and rice processing. Consequently, many farmers with less than one hectare of
land were unable to cover production costs and still
have sufficient rice for home consumption. Also a
majority of the farmers are reportedly behind on their
irrigation loan payments. In addition to the debt for
their pumps, farmers are paying for electricity to run
the pumps and for the increased fertilizer, improved
seeds and pesticides. With the failure of the price of
rice to rise it is feared that a time will come when
some of the farmers' costs will equal or exceed their
incomes.[4]

According to the Project Evaluation Report, although
the Philippine irrigation project has been a success in
terms of total output, and the projects have assisted
the country in reaching self-sufficiency in rice, in-
sufficient attention was paid to marketing support,
technical assistance, land tenure and land rents. For
example, the landlord's percentage of gross yield re-
mains the same with higher output, while the landlord
does not incur the costs of the irrigation systems.
There is also a need to improve the system of rural
credit. It is interesting to note, however, that the
Philippine government not only supports the price of
rice above the world market level, but subsidizes

certain inputs such as the price of fertilizer.

The major lesson from the implementation of the Philippine irrigation program is that attention must be paid to a number of problems in small-scale agriculture other than a program to increase output. Could it be that given the structure of small farming in the assisted area rice production is simply not economical under current methods of production?

Beginning in 1974 AID contributed $25.7 million to an irrigation program in Korea for the purpose of assisting that country in becoming self-sufficient in rice and barley and for raising farm incomes. The project made only a marginal contribution to rice self-sufficiency as this was achieved by 1975, soon after the project was initiated, and it did not help improve barley production since it actually declined due to the high government support prices for rice and the growing demand for wheat in urban areas.

According to the AID Project Impact Evaluation Report, the project succeeded in increasing rice yields some 50 to 75 percent and new rice lands were brought into production. Farm income objectives were also met from rice alone, with the exception of very small and part-time farmers. However, the success of the program depended heavily on the fact that the Korean government maintained a rice support price of more than double world prices.[5] Although the project focused entirely on irrigation, "it basically succeeded where many similar projects in other societies failed. This success may be attributed to efficient technical management, and effective concomitant delivery of a wide variety of agricultural inputs and services, conditions absent in many parts of the world."[6] "Fertilizer, pest management, chemicals, tillers, sprayers, improved seed and production credit are widely available. They have been necessary to the project's success. Furthermore, the farmers know, or have been taught, how to use effectively these materials and have been motivated to do so."

The government subsidizes both the operating and capital costs of the irrigation systems. Hence, unlike the Philippine program discussed above, farm incomes are increased and the debt obligations on the irrigation systems covered. However, Korean consumers and taxpayers are paying a substantial price for Korean self-sufficiency in rice in contrast to importing rice at world market prices. The question arises whether the external social benefits from the system justifies the cost, or whether it would be more economic to allow a restructuring of the Korean agricultural sector which might enable agriculture to pay its own way.

Causes of Failures of Aid-Supported
Agricultural Programs

In reviewing the appraisals of aid-supported agricultural programs, the most frequently mentioned cause
of failure to achieve the objectives of the program
has been the pricing policies followed by governments
who tend to prevent farm prices from rising to free
market levels in order to hold down the cost of living.
The lack of price incentives impairs the willingness
of farmers even to participate in the programs, since
they usually must pay for inputs out of revenue or
funds borrowed from the credit agencies. On the other
hand, successful programs achieved by means of subsidized product prices and prices of farm inputs raise
questions with regard to the net social benefits of
programs designed to maintain a basically inefficient
agricultural structure based on very small farms.

The second most frequently mentioned cause of
failure has been the inadequacy of institutional arrangements and the shortage of qualified extension personnel
for transferring technology to the farmers. This was
cited by a recent US General Accounting Office study
as the principal reason for the slow progress in transferring improved technology for increasing agricultural
production in Egypt.[7] The large AID program has apparently been successful in dealing with some of the difficult technical problems faced by Egyptian agriculture, but the transfer of this technology has been
impaired by a "lack of linkages between research and
extension" and by the inadequacy of the extension
staff.[8]

A third criticism of many aid-supported agricultural programs is that they have not resulted in the
creation of an efficient institutional structure within
the government or in the private sector to implement
the initial aid-supported programs, or to continue to
function beyond the intitial programs once the aid
funds have been disbursed. Aid for self-sustaining
growth should, of course, serve to establish institutions that will continue to promote agricultural progress in the initial target area and to provide material
inputs, credit and technical services to a growing
number of farmers in the country after the aid funds
have been disbursed. This means, among other things,
a commitment on the part of the government to fund the
institutional and extension services component of the
program, to provide the foreign exchange for the purchase
of imported agricultural inputs, and to establish credit
institutions that will not simply transfer the funds
provided for foreign aid, but will mobilize domestic
capital for use by the agricultural sector. In some
countries external support for agricultural credit may
be questionable since it seeks to correct a distortion

of governmental budget allocation and allocation of domestic capital. However, it might be justified as seed money to help establish a permanent system of agricultural credit available on reasonable terms to small farmers who have not had access to existing financial institutions.

In a recent book, Aart van de Laar, a former World Bank official, raises serious questions regarding aid-supported agricultural programs for the distribution of credits at concessional interest rates. Moreover, he suggests that the bulk of these institutional credits go to the relatively better-off farmers, traders and middlemen rather than to the small farmers in greatest need of credit.[9]

By and large the most successful aid-supported agricultural programs have been those which have reached a large number of small farmers with appropriate technical packages and accompanied by government price policies that provide incentives for small farmer participation. Such programs have achieved a greater increase in agricultural output and have been more cost effective than programs directed to agricultural cooperatives and government plantations. However, we suspect that many of the programs designed to assist farms of uneconomic size may not be cost effective. Aid in support of social programs and land reform as opposed to directly productive programs have not been especially successful. Land reform is probably too politically sensitive to be tackled by external agencies.

INDUSTRIAL IMPORT LOANS AND GENERAL PROGRAM LOANS

A number of countries have received a series of concessionary loans from the World Bank or IDA to finance imports of industrial raw materials, spare parts and other industrial inputs. Since the programs are not specifically designed to promote new industries or to influence the pattern of industrial development, there is little to distinguish them from balance of payments loans. Some countries have received such loans year after year with little progress in moving the countries toward equilibrium through expanding their industrial exports. Moreover, as long as the country can count on additional loans of this type, there is no reason for it to undertake the necessary policy reforms to improve its balance of payments position.

The same may be said of general program loans not specifically related to a particular sector. This does not mean that under some circumstances program loans cannot serve a very useful purpose, as was the case for example in two program loans to Korea (one in 1975 and the other in 1976) which assisted that country in

overcoming balance of payments problems accompanying
the sharp rise in oil prices. Nevertheless, these were
not development loans with a strong institution building
component. Some of the earlier program-type loans to
Korea when that country was emerging from the war with
North Korea provided a rapid and timely supplement to
its domestic savings. Together with favorable economic
policies and a generally good social and institutional
base for development, these loans helped to achieve a
rapid increase in Korea's growth rate during the 1960-
1970 period. However, the successful outcome of program
loans to Korea is scarcely a tribute to the effectiveness of program loans for influencing development strategy by the donors. Korea was doing the right things
before the loans were made!

In some cases program loans or sector program
loans such as loans for industrial imports have been
made in conjunction with IMF standby credits, so that,
in effect, the foreign exchange provided by the loans
from development assistance agencies simply supplemented
the IMF credits. Without necessarily condemning such
financing, we believe that it constitutes balance of
payments financing rather than true development financing assistance in the sense we are using the term.

LOANS TO DEVELOPMENT FINANCE CORPORATIONS (DFCs)

Substantial amounts of both multilateral and bilateral loans have gone to DFCs for making sub-loans
to industrial enterprises and to other economic sectors
as well. With few exceptions the DFCs themselves are
operated by the government while their sub-loans go
mainly to private firms; some sub-loans are made to
government enterprises or mixed enterprises. Although
there are certainly cases where loans to DFCs have made
a positive contribution to achieving a condition of
self-sustained growth, e.g., the loans to the (private)
Korean Development Finance Corporation, most of the
loan appraisals that we have reviewed point to several
serious criticisms from the standpoint of their contribution to self-sustained growth. First, most DFCs
have not succeeded in raising sufficient capital from
the private capital markets to enable them eventually
to replace external loan capital with domestic capital.
Some DFCs have relied year after year for well over a
decade on loans from foreign assistance agencies without
tapping the domestic capital market. In some cases these
DFCs are not permitted by the government to pay interest
rates high enough to attract domestic capital. It is
sometimes argued that DFCs provide foreign exchange for
imports which cannot be provided by the domestic capital
market because of exchange controls. This then makes
the DFCs channels for allocating foreign exchange rather

than intermediaries for allocating capital funds derived from domestic savers. The continued availability of external development loans for this purpose has often failed to promote reforms of the capital and foreign exchange markets and has probably served to perpetuate the existing system.

Another criticism of many of the DFCs supported by external development financing is that the DFCs have failed to diversify their operations to areas outside the main urban centers and have not assisted or promoted new firms in getting started. Moreover, little effort has been made to direct credits to export-oriented industries. In other words, external funds are passed through by the DFCs without promoting a development strategy aimed at self-sustained growth.

What is needed for promoting the flow of domestic capital into the most productive uses is the development of a free capital market in which private financial intermediaries play a major role. Government financial institutions have in general not been successful in mobilizing domestic capital and allocating it to the highest priority uses. The International Financial Corporation is perhaps best equipped to provide external capital, technical assistance, and promotional activities in this field.

LOANS FOR POWER AND TRANSPORTATION

Loans for large power and transportation projects still constitute a substantial portion of the loan portfolio of multilateral development institutions. They are perhaps the easiest to make from the standpoint of staff involvement per million dollars of disbursements. Although sometimes projections of the demand for services rendered by the projects have proved overly optimistic or there have been technical errors in the engineering, or the projects have suffered from inadequate maintenance after completion, by and large such projects have yielded an acceptable rate of social return. However, the appraisal reports show that in many cases financial returns from power and other projects, the services of which are sold, have been quite low and not sufficient for capital replacement. In this sense they are not promoting self-sustained development. Since there is a large consumption content in power and transportation services, inadequate tariffs mean subsidizing consumption as well as providing services below cost to industry and agriculture. Moreover, there is often a misallocation of capital, such as building excellent freeways between urban centers without feeder roads to the rural sectors.

It should be possible to select power and transportation projects for aid support which would remove serious bottlenecks for expanding agricultural and industrial activity, while leaving to the governments the more politically attractive projects which the governments are likely to undertake on their own. What we are suggesting is that aid-supported infrastructure projects be selected on the basis of their unique contribution to directly productive activities and of the likelihood of their being self-supported in the future.

Projects for meeting increased demands for power in large urban cities in developing countries are almost sure to be financed by governments if loans from development assistance agencies are not forthcoming to finance them. Modern urban cities are simply not viable without power, telephones and other services associated with modern living. Such projects provide a convenient way of supplementing the resources of developing coun-tries and there may also be a development component from project appraisal and technical assistance by the aid agency. However, much of the power goes to improving the level of living of the middle class. Hence, their contribution to industrial output may be small in relation to the cost. The availability of external loans from development assistance agencies may in some cases have the effect of enabling government-owned power companies to avoid charging rates high enough to expand power generation or borrowing funds for expansion on commercial terms.

Since governments frequently neglect infrastructure in smaller towns, "rural electrification" has become a popular target for development assistance agencies de-sirous of improving the conditions in rural areas. However, questions arise regarding the contribution of such programs to self-sustained growth. The conclusions of AID appraisals of rural electrification loans to two Latin American countries are illuminating.

AID made two loans in 1973 and 1974 for rural electification in Bolivia designed to improve social and economic conditions in rural areas adjacent to six urban areas. It was assumed that the availability of electric power would stimulate the development of rural industry and irrigation as well as improve social conditions through residential and public service usage of electricity. The conclusion of the AID Project Impact Evaluation Report was that "The preponderant positive impact of the rural electrification projects was social....Electric power did not seem to play a catalytic role in the economic development of rural areas nor to be a precondition for it."[10] Where rural industry and irrigation development has occurred, it has been accomplished by self-generating diesel systems in response to price incentives and other factors such as the availability of credit and technical assistance."[11] Moreover, the evaluation report points out that the utilities are unlikely to expand adequately to the growing demand for household connections. The aid-supported program does not appear to have a replicating or self-generating character.

The evaluation of several AID-supported rural electrification programs in Ecuador between 1964 and 1975 reached somewhat similar conclusions.[12] Electrification had only a minor effect on industrial production and none on agriculture. The impact on social services outside of market towns was modest. The evaluation report does not give rural electrification a high priority for the development of market towns and service centers in Ecuador, and suggests "AID involvement may best be restricted to technical assistance and training rather than hardware. Indeed, while safe water, roads, and education or basic facilities may have a high claim on development resources, the development of a market town in the year 1980 can hardly be imagined without a reliable supply of electricity. The only significant issue in market town electrification is not whether to electrify, but when and how."[13]

The evaluation report also points out that electric power in Ecuador is grossly underpriced because the price of fuel is not only a small fraction of the world price, but less than one-third its cost of production in Ecuador. This suggests that the electric power produced by projects which are mainly enjoyed by the higher income people constitutes a substantial subsidy to consumption.[14]

EDUCATION, HEALTH AND OTHER SOCIAL PROGRAMS

A certain level of formal education and training is undoubtedly a precondition for achieving sustained growth. Raising the skills of the least developed countries to a level consistent with self-sustained growth will require at least a generation and a continuously rising budgetary commitment by domestic governmental entities. Foreign assistance for education has gone in large part for physical infrastructure with concentration on the critical area of secondary education and technical training. The most important contribution that foreign aid can make to education is in the training of teachers and administrators both domestically and abroad, and in the design of the curriculum to meet manpower needs for development. Assistance in institution building rather than the creation of physical infrastructure should be the primary objective of foreign aid to education. Hence, the emphasis of aid to education should be technical assistance rather than budget support for buildings which nearly all governments are capable of erecting.

Much of the same may be said regarding other social

programs in the fields of health, sanitation, low-cost
housing, and other community services and facilities.
In very poor countries a minimum of decent living
conditions and community services is essential for
productivity and can be justified in terms of its
contribution to growth. However, the commitment of
governments and community organizations to social programs is indispensable to their success, and local
entities should provide those components they are best
capable of providing with their own resources.

NOTES

1 AID Project Impact Evaluation Report No.1,
Colombia: Small Farmer Market Access, Washington, DC:
AID, December 1979.

2 AID Project Impact Evaluation Report No. 13,
Rural Roads in Thailand, Washington, DC: AID, December
1980.

3 "Impact of the Bank's Rural Development Lending,"
Finance and Development, September 1975, pp. 24-28.

4 AID Project Impact Evalutation Report No. 4,
Philippine Small-Scale Irrigation, Washington, DC: AID,
May 1980.

5 AID Project Impact Evalutation Report No. 12,
Korean Irrigation, Washington, DC: AID, December 1980.

6 Ibid., p. 5.

7 U.S. Assistance to Egyptian Agriculture: Slow
Progress After Five Years, Washington, DC: US General
Accounting Office, March 16, 1981.

8 Ibid., p. 20.

9 The World Bank and the Poor, Boston: Martinus,
Nijhoff Publishing, 1980, pp. 158-164.

10 AID Project Impact Evaluation Report No. 16,
Bolivia: Rural Electrification, Washington, DC: AID,
December 1980, p. iv.

11 AID Project Impact Evaluation Report No. 16,
op.cit., p. iv.

12 AID Project Impact Evaluation Report No. 21,
Ecuador: Rural Electrification, Washington, DC: AID,
June 1981.

13 AID Project Impact Evaluation Report No. 21, Ecuador: Rural Electrification, Washington, DC: AID, June 1981. p. 14.

14 AID Project Impact Evaluation Report No. 16, op.cit., p. 14.

7
Findings and Conclusions

A number of generalizations, findings and conclusions were given in the course of the preceding chapters, some of which have only an indirect relation to the principal issues raised in the Work Statement. In this chapter we organize our principal findings and conclusions in terms of the major issues and questions on which we were specifically asked to comment by the Work Statement.

1. What Can the Theory and Evidence on Economic Development Tell Us About the Role of Foreign Aid in Assisting Developing Countries in Achieving a Condition of Self-Sustained Growth?

Our review of the development literature in Chapters 1 and 2 covering the past 30 years reveals substantial changes in the theory of economic development and considerable progress in our understanding of the development process, achieved in large measure by intensive studies of the experience of individual developing countries. The rather simple economic growth models that portrayed growth mainly as a function of capital investment, the level of which is constrained by domestic saving and capital imports, have given way to highly complex models which include both the characteristics of the socio-economic base for development and a number of economic variables, many of which are subject to control by policy instruments. Total factor productivity has become a major explanatory factor in growth, which in turn is a function of many variables, including the level and composition of skills, incentives, technology, the allocation of investment, and the general economic environment created by monetary, fiscal and other governmental policies. Among the primary determinants of economic growth are the policies of government, the dedication of a country's leaders to national economic progress, and the quality of personnel in private and governmental organizations

for carrying out growth-creating activities. Capital
investment continues to be essential for growth,
whether derived from domestic savings or from external
flows, but capital contributes to growth only in close
relationship with the dynamic human, institutional and
governmental factors mentioned above.

In assisting developing countries to achieve a
condition of self-sustaining growth, concessionary aid
provided by development institutions has a number of
functions, the nature and relative importance of which
depend upon the stage of development progress reached
by the indivdual country. These stages are characterized
under Question 2 below, and the functions of concessionary aid relating to each stage are discussed under
Question 4.

Development theory has benefitted from a number of
country studies that have emphasized the relationship
between economic growth and domestic economic policy.
Development economists have made important advances in
analyzing the effects of alternative domestic policies
on resource allocation and growth. These domestic policies include trade and exchange rate policies, monetary,
fiscal and credit policies, and policies relating to
capital markets and price investment incentives.

The shift in the development objectives by AID,
the World Bank, DAC, and other organizations concerned
with promoting development from major emphasis on growth
to that of reducing the incidence of absolute poverty
has led a number of development economists to investigate
whether and to what degree there exists a conflict
between maximizing growth and meeting basic human needs.
In our review of the extensive development literature
on this question we conclude that little or no conflict
exists between the two objectives. Much of the poverty
of developing countries can be traced to unemployment
or employment in very low productivity activities, and
the bulk of the absolute poverty is found in the poor,
slow growing countries. If these countries are to make
substantial progress toward the condition of self-
sustaining growth, the principal objective of development policy must be that of bringing a high proportion
of the workforce into productive employment. Moreover,
there is considerable statistical evidence that raising
the per capita GNP of poor countries reduces the
proportion of absolute poor.

In the course of our literature survey we dealt
briefly with the studies of a minority of development
economists that have sought to show that virtually all
foreign aid either makes no contribution to development
or is counterproductive. Much of this aid pessimism is
based on a statistical demonstration that capital imports
reduce savings. In reviewing the theoretical and statistical studies supporting the position of the aid pessimists, we find flaws in both their analysis and their

statistical methodology. Although there are undoubtedly cases in which foreign aid has proved to be of little value in promoting growth, there is ample evidence that aid provided under the proper conditions and responses of the recipients can be a powerful stimulant to growth and to the establishment of the preconditions for self-sustained growth.

2. How Should Development Progress Be Measured?

A country may have various development objectives which may be realized by alternative policies and programs for the allocation of its resources. But whatever these objectives may be in terms of alternative social programs, a country's ability to realize them will depend largely on the growth of its total output of goods and services. Hence, the most important single measure of development progress is the rate of growth in per capita GNP. However, GNP growth should be broadly based on the sense of covering many economic sectors and regions and should not simply reflect a rapid rise in a few primary export commodities. Broadly based growth is essential for providing opportunities for productive employment.

We have already indicated that we see no basic conflict between growth and the reduction of absolute poverty, and as long as countries do not adopt measures that will impair incentives or deliberately increase overall consumption at the expense of investment for growth, a higher level of output will provide the flexibility necessary to achieve a number of particular social goals. Therefore we believe that the goal of promoting self-sustained growth is the correct one for development institutions. If countries pursue policies and practices that impair the achievement of self-sustained grwoth, it will simply prolong, perhaps indefinitely, the period during which they will require concessionary aid in order to maintain economic viability.

In Chapter 3, we defined the condition of self-sustained growth in quantitative terms. Although our definition of this condition as a rate of per capita GNP growth of 2.5 percent per annum and a minimum per capita GNP base in the range of $800 to $1000 in 1980 dollars is admittedly arbitrary, we believe it is necessary to have some quantitative standard if the goal is to be operational from the standpoint of aid administration. We also believe that the suggested per capita income base is a minimum standard and we have not argued against the provision of World Bank-type loans for countries with higher per capita incomes.

We have also identified several stages in progress towards self-sustained growth. The first stage is that represented by the more primitive economies of sub-

Saharan Africa in which the vast bulk of the population
is illiterate, agricultural productivity is very low
and output stagnating, there is little infrastructure
outside the urban centers, and there are virtually no
institutions for transferring technology and other inputs required for agricultural progress to the rural
population. At this stage few preconditions for sustained growth exist.

The second stage is represented by the countries of
the Indian subcontinent where there exists a core of
technically trained people, 20-40 percent of the adult
population is literate, there is considerable infrastructure and import substituting industry, and progress
has been made in raising agricultural output through
the introduction of modern technology, seeds, fertilizer
and irrigation. At this stage some but not all of the
preconditions for sustained growth have been achieved.

A third stage is represented by a number of Latin
American countries which have many if not most of the
preconditions for self-sustained growth. Some of these
countries at this stage are growing satisfactorily, but
require larger amounts of external capital than they are
able to obtain from nonconcessionary sources to maintain
their growth rates and to achieve a condition of self-
sustained growth. Other countries are not performing
satisfactorily as a consequence of poor governmental
policies.

A fourth stage is represented by countries that
are growing satisfactorily and have a per capita GNP
above $1000 in 1980 dollars. Nevertheless, some of
these countries have experienced aborted growth as a
consequence of external shocks or poor domestic policies,
and, in addition, have experienced serious external debt
problems during the past decade.

The above categories relate principally to progress
toward the capacity for self-sustained growth as determined by the preconditions. The actual growth performance of a country at any stage in the capacity for
growth will be determined in substantial measure by its
domestic policies. Domestic policies also affect progress toward acquiring the preconditions for sustained
growth. Finally, domestic policies affect the ability
of a country with the capacity for sustained growth to
obtain nonconcessionary external capital.

3. What Should Be the Role of Government in Achieving Successful Development and How Can Government Policies Inhibit the Effectiveness of Foreign Aid?

A number of case studies of developing countries
have shown a clear relationship between growth and the
pursuit of outward-oriented policies, including exchange
rates that maintain a proper relationship between internal and external prices, free domestic capital markets,

and the absence of controls on prices and investment. These same policies also play a role in achieving the preconditions for sustained growth.

We have provided a number of examples showing how concessionary aid has been ineffective or less effective in promoting conditions of self-sustained growth because of improper governmental policies. Inadequate price incentives have frequently reduced the participation of farmers in aid-supported agricultural projects and programs; assistance to DFCs has failed to create self-sustaining financial institutions based on the mobilization of domestic capital as a consequence of government controls over interest rates; and concessionary aid to industry has failed to expand exports as a consequence of overvalued exchange rates and trade restrictions.

In establishing the preconditions for sustained growth, governments must do much more than adopt laissez faire policies and create a favorable economic environment for domestic and foreign investment. Government agencies must play a role in institution building for delivering aid-supported inputs such as technical assistance, seed, fertilizer, credit, and irrigation for modernizing agriculture in the private sector and in allocating capital for infrastructure projects in the public sector in a manner that is most conducive to growth. Governments must also contribute to the creation of human capital by providing education and health facilities; such facilities are often neglected in the poorer agricultural areas.

Policies with respect to government-operated utilities and transportation also have an important impact on the effectiveness of concessionary aid to the public sector. For example, a government power company should charge rates sufficient not only to cover operating and capital costs, but should generate funds for their expansion or replication if such aid-supported projects are to contribute to self-generating growth. In the case of projects such as feeder roads and other infrastructure important to agricultural development that are supported by concessionary aid, their maintenance and expansion to other areas should be provided for in governmental budgets if the programs are to contribute to self-generating growth.

Production by government enterprises in industry, mining and export agriculture has usually been characterized by a relatively high degree of inefficiency, in part because of political interference with management. Mining is a conspicuous example since efficient foreign-owned mining enterprises have frequently been nationalized with a consequent decline in productivity. Although it is recognized that in some countries there may be no alternative to public operation of enterprises in certain industries, free entry by private domestic and foreign investors should be maintained on a non-discriminatory basis for all industrial and mining activities.

4. What is the Role of Concessionary Aid In Development? How Can It Be Made More Effective In Promoting Self-Sustained Growth, and Under What Conditions May It Be Less Effective or Even Counterproductive?

Concessionary aid for development has two fundamental roles. First, it provides external resources to countries in amounts beyond which they can obtain from nonconcessionary sources without overburdening their debt service capacity. Second, concessionary aid (when properly administered) provides donor guidance on development strategy, project formulation and appraisal, and technical assistance in promoting the preconditions for sustained growth. The relative importance of these contributions to the promotion of self-sustained growth tends to differ with the stage of progress toward this goal. During the first stage identified in Question 2 above, concessionary aid should have a large technical assistance and training component, with substantial emphasis on institution building for the transfer of essential inputs to farmers for increasing agricultural output. In the second stage development guidance, institution building and technical assistance should also constitute important components of concessionary aid, but the role of supplementing domestic resources for basic infrastructure and for the nonagricultural productive sectors become more important.

In the third stage in which most of the preconditions for sustained growth have been achieved, development guidance in the form of project formulation and appraisal plus technical assistance is still important, but the major role of concessionary aid is providing sufficient external resources for maintaining a relatively high growth rate until the full conditions for self-sustained growth have been achieved. These full conditions mean that the country is able to obtain the external resources required for maintaining a relatively high growth rate from nonconcessionary sources.

Where concessionary aid is provided in the fourth stage in which the capacity for self-generating growth is fully achieved and demonstrated for a period of time, a development component in the form of guidance on development strategies and in project and program formulation and appraisal should be retained. At no stage should concessionary aid for development simply provide a source of external capital or balance of payments or budget support without a development component.

In each of the four stages the provision of concessionary aid should be conditioned on the adoption by the government of appropriate policies for achieving

and maintaining self-sustained growth. Without appropriate policies, aid is likely to prove less than
fully effective or, at worst, it may prolong policies
that inhibit the achievement of self-sustained growth.
For example, continued balance of payments support
without appropriate policy reform and the proper allocation of fiscal resources may encourage a country
to put off politically difficult reforms.

So far as possible, aid-supported projects and
programs should provide their own maintenance and replication from domestic resources. In other words, self-
generating growth should be built into aid-supported
projects themselves.

5. How Should Development Assistance Be Allo-cated to Maximize Its Effectiveness in Promoting Self-Sustained Growth?

A. ODA should be provided solely to countries
with very low per capita incomes. These countries have
the least capacity for obtaining external capital from
nonconcessionary sources or even for servicing loans,
such as World Bank loans, with a relatively small grant
element. The possibilities for increasing per capita
incomes of large numbers of people in the more populous
poor countries are very great, and increasing the growth
rates of these countries has been found to be the most
effective means of reducing the incidence of absolute
poverty in the Third World. In addition to limiting
ODA to LDCs with very low per capita incomes, there
should be maximum per capita eligibility requirements
for all types of concessionary aid.

B. Support for social projects and infrastructure
should be limited to those projects that can be justified
in terms of their contribution to growth. In particular,
support of infrastructure projects that mainly provide
services to middle-class urban populations should be
avoided.

C. Major emphasis should be given to projects and
programs that increase employment and productivity in the
private sector, including infrastructure that removes
bottlenecks or provides incentives for private sector
activities.

D. Wherever possible within the limits of the
politico-economic structure of the country, support for
government enterprises operating in industry and agriculture should be avoided in favor of IFC assistance
to the private sector. However, there are serious
difficulties with direct concessionary aid to the private
sector. Risk absorption rather than interest subsidies
should be the principal means of assisting the private

sector, and venture capital can be provided by the IFC.

E. Development assistance in the form of general program loans and loans to finance industrial imports have in general been less effective in promoting growth activities than loans for specific projects and programs in which there is direct donor agency involvement. Although experience with World Bank and IDA balance of payments loans for structural adjustment is too short to pass judgment, their resemblance to the program loans of the past raises serious questions regarding the probability of their effectiveness.

The case against general program-type loans is admittedly a controversial one, especially since examples of successful ones in terms of the policies pursued by the recipients can be cited. Our questioning of general program loans arises in part from the fact that balance of payments assistance is basically the province of the IMF, which is concerned with macro-economic policies such as fiscal, monetary and exchange rate policies, which policies constitute the key to balance of payments adjustment. It is true that international development lending institutions are concerned with the internal allocation of resources among economic sectors such as agriculture, industry and infrastructure, and the appropriate allocation of investment to the export industries. But on the basis of the experience of these lending agencies, we question whether general balance of payments loans accompanied by an agreement to pursue policies relating to price incentives, trade controls, and private and foreign investment required to promote an appropriate allocation of resources for successful development are likely to prove effective. Very often the loan proceeds are spent for covering balance of payments deficits well before the policy reforms can be adopted if, indeed, they ever are adopted. An alternative is to make multiple project and sectoral program loans, the employment of which is conditioned on the adoption of specific policies necessary to achieve the objectives of the loans. As regards the broader policies required for successful development, their adoption should be taken into account by the lending agency in determining whether the prospective borrower has met the performance criteria for loan eligibility.

Index

103